I0418347

MASTERING EMOTIONAL INTELLIGENCE & BUILDING MENTAL TOUGHNESS

Maximize Your Potential: Elevate Personal Growth and Achieve Peak Performance through Self-Awareness, Resilience, and Confidence

AMBER PRESTON

© **Copyright 2024 - All rights reserved.**

The content contained within this book may not be reproduced, duplicated or transmitted without direct written permission from the author or the publisher.

Under no circumstances will any blame or legal responsibility be held against the publisher, or author, for any damages, reparation, or monetary loss due to the information contained within this book, either directly or indirectly.

Legal Notice:

This book is copyright protected. It is only for personal use. You cannot amend, distribute, sell, use, quote or paraphrase any part, or the content within this book, without the consent of the author or publisher.

Disclaimer Notice:

Please note the information contained within this document is for educational and entertainment purposes only. All effort has been executed to present accurate, up to date, reliable, complete information. No warranties of any kind are declared or implied. Readers acknowledge that the author is not engaged in the rendering of legal, financial, medical or professional advice. The content within this book has been derived from various sources. Please consult a licensed professional before attempting any techniques outlined in this book.

By reading this document, the reader agrees that under no circumstances is the author responsible for any losses, direct or indirect, that are incurred as a result of the use of the information contained within this document, including, but not limited to, errors, omissions, or inaccuracies.

Table of Contents

Mastering Emotional Intelligence with Ease

Building Mental Toughness

Mastering Emotional Intelligence with Ease

7 STEP GUIDE TO ELEVATE YOUR PERSONAL
GROWTH BY IMPROVING SELF-AWARENESS,
BUILDING EMOTIONAL RESILIENCE, AND
ENHANCING YOUR SOCIAL SKILLS

KICKSTART YOUR JOURNEY TOWARDS MASTERING EMOTIONAL INTELLIGENCE NOW!

You're already off to a great start on working towards a better you by grabbing a copy of this book!

As a way of saying thank you for your purchase, I am offering a FREE companion Self-Reflection Workbook. This workbook accompanies the lessons taught in Chapter 2, as a hands-on guide to prioritizing you!

But it's more than just a workbook; it's a part of your personal journey, emphasizing the skills you need to master emotional intelligence with ease.

To get the free workbook, <u>click here</u> or scan the QR code below with your mobile phone!

Introduction

Imagine a tornado tearing through a quiet town, uprooting trees, destroying homes, and causing utter chaos in its path. It's wild, unpredictable, and leaves a trail of devastation. Now, imagine that tornado within you—a maelstrom of emotions, whirling and colliding, each gust stronger than the last, leaving you feeling lost and overwhelmed. That, my friend, is the storm of our emotions without the compass of emotional intelligence.

Have you ever wondered why some days you feel utterly crushed by even the smallest hiccup, while on others you can navigate life's challenges with grace and ease? Or how one comment can cause a heated argument, while another day, the same comment rolls off like water off a duck's back?

If so, it's not just you. This book is for the countless souls who've felt the same way: the feeling that emotions rule their days, the constant struggle to understand others, and the yearning for deeper, more meaningful relationships. You didn't pick up this book by chance. Something prompted you, a catalyst. Perhaps it was a failed relationship, a challenging workplace environment, or simply a burning desire to know yourself better.

Now, imagine a world where you can

- truly understand the intricacies of your own emotions and those of others.
- navigate social situations with grace, ease, and genuine connection.
- bounce back from setbacks with renewed vigor and strength.
- engage in enriching and fulfilling relationships.

Doesn't that sound like a dream?

It's no surprise that icons like Oprah Winfrey and Elon Musk credit their success, in part, to their high emotional intelligence. Their ability to connect, understand, and motivate not just themselves but also those around them sets them apart in a world brimming with talent.

By the time you turn the last page, you'll have uncovered

- the underlying principles of emotional intelligence and their profound impact.
- strategies to enhance your self-awareness.
- the pillars of emotional resilience.
- techniques to foster effective communication and social skills.
- insights into cultivating empathy.
- the art of managing relationships for a harmonious life.
- the transformative professional implications of emotional intelligence.

Before these insights were available, many wandered in the dark, grappling with relationships and self-worth, unable to harness the full potential of their emotions. Now, armed with the knowledge in this book, you are set to embark on a transformative journey.

You might wonder why you should heed the guidance within these pages. This book is the culmination of extensive research, real-life experiences, and insights from experts in the field of psychology and emotional intelligence. It's not just a compilation of theories; it's a testament to the countless individuals who've transformed their lives by harnessing the power of their emotions.

Let's be honest; the internet is flooded with information. You could spend hours, days, or even years sifting through articles, attending seminars, and joining workshops. But here, you're presented with a distilled version, a roadmap, cutting through the noise and pointing you toward the core of what truly matters.

Recall the most profound moments in your life. Can you see the thread of emotion weaving through them? The euphoria of achievements, the heartbreak of lost love, the comfort of a friend's embrace, the sting of harsh words. Our lives are colored by our emotions, and this book will help you to develop strategies to be the best, most emotionally intelligent version of yourself.

So, let's journey together through the landscapes of our emotions and discover the harmony that awaits. With every chapter, with every page, you'll move closer to a life where emotions are not a tumultuous storm but a gentle guiding breeze. Welcome to your new beginning.

ONE

Step #1—Understanding Emotional Intelligence

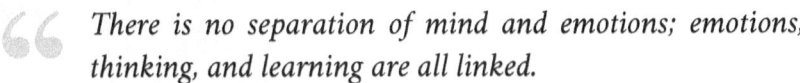 *There is no separation of mind and emotions; emotions, thinking, and learning are all linked.*

Eric Jensen

Isn't it fascinating how intertwined our thoughts and feelings truly are? Eric Jensen's words echo a truth we've all felt but might not have put into words. We've all had those moments when a sudden emotion shifts our entire perspective or when a deep thought tugs at our heartstrings. This dance between what we feel and think is the essence of emotional intelligence.

Emotional intelligence is not just a buzzword. It's a transformative skill set, a paradigm shift that touches every facet of our lives. From professional advancements to personal well-being, its ripple effect is profound. Cultivating emotional intelligence is akin to investing in oneself, promising a brighter, more fulfilling, and harmonious future.

So, what's the big deal about emotional intelligence? Why not just stick to the good old IQ? Well, let's think of it this way: Imagine navigating through life's ups and downs without truly understanding why we feel the way we do or how those feelings drive our decisions. Sounds challenging, right? That's where this chapter comes in, providing clarity and insight into the world of emotional intelligence.

Ready to dive deep? Let's get started exploring the relationship between our minds and emotions and discovering the true power of emotional intelligence in our lives.

My aim? By the end of this chapter, you won't just have a textbook definition. Instead, you'll have a deep, intuitive understanding that will serve as your compass for the rest of our journey together.

Defining Emotional Intelligence

Emotional intelligence, often referred to as EQ (Emotional Quotient), is the capacity to recognize, understand, manage, and effectively use emotions in both ourselves and others. This entails not only being aware of our own emotions and those of others but also understanding how those emotions drive behaviors and how to apply this understanding in various situations. In essence, it's about being emotionally aware and using that awareness to navigate our interactions in a thoughtful and effective manner (Cherry, 2023; *Emotional Intelligence Toolkit*, n.d.; Mental Health America, n.d.).

Can Everyone Have Emotional Intelligence?

A common concern is whether emotional intelligence is an innate trait or something that can be developed. Here's the reassuring news: While it's been found that only about 36% of individuals can accurately identify their emotions as they happen (*Are You Emotionally Intelligent?*, n.d.), this doesn't mean that the rest lack the capacity for emotional intelligence.

Not everyone might start with high emotional intelligence skills right out of the gate, but everyone possesses the potential to hone and develop these strengths. Just like many abilities in life, building one's EQ isn't necessarily about being born with it but about consistent practice, awareness, and effort. So, if you're concerned about not having a natural aptitude for EQ, remember that emotional intelligence can be cultivated and enhanced with dedication and intention (Schwantes, 2021).

Emotional intelligence stands as a beacon in the realm of personal development and workplace efficiency. With an array of benefits to its name, let's delve deeper into each one to better understand its profound impact.

Reduces Stress

In both personal and professional life, emotional intelligence serves as a shield against the pressures and stresses of the day. Recognizing and managing stress early can lead to a more balanced approach to life's challenges, ultimately improving your physical health as well. Reduced stress promotes longevity and boosts energy and motivation, which is beneficial both at home and at work. Furthermore, lower stress levels can improve family relationships and make social interactions more enjoyable. On the job, less stress means better focus, increased productivity, and a healthier work-life balance. Less stress in your personal life can even make you a more patient and understanding colleague, forming a virtuous cycle.

Improves Communication Skills

Effective communication is vital both in personal relationships and the workplace. Emotional intelligence helps in reading non-verbal cues and actively listening, thus reducing misunderstandings and fostering fruitful interactions. It also improves your intrapersonal communication, allowing you to operate from a place of self-belief and confidence. Enhanced communication can lead to stronger relationships with friends and family, and it can also boost your performance in team settings at work. Clear communication also means fewer conflicts, which can make your personal and professional life more harmonious. Furthermore, a positive internal dialogue reinforces self-confidence, making challenges easier to face in any environment.

Enhances Social Skills

Social skills are not just for team meetings or casual get-togethers; they are essential for quality interactions in every area of life. High emotional intelligence provides the tools for understanding social scenarios, facilitating effective team collaborations, and enhancing interpersonal relationships. Such skills make you approachable in any setting and a consensus builder in the professional world. In personal life, these skills can deepen friendships and familial relationships by improving mutual understanding and empathy. In the professional setting, individuals with better social skills often find it easier to lead teams and manage projects effectively. Moreover, understanding social cues can help you better navigate complicated social situations both at work and in your personal life.

Creates a Positive Environment

People with high EQ often create nurturing and positive environments, both at home and at work. These atmospheres not only enhance job satisfaction but also make personal relationships more meaningful. In such environments, conflicts are resolved amicably, and the overall morale remains high. A positive environment at home contributes to emotional well-being, which in turn reflects positively at work. Likewise, a harmonious workplace can reduce stress and make your personal life more peaceful. The skills you gain from creating a positive environment at work can also be applied to improve your home life, leading to a more satisfying and integrated life experience.

Specific Benefits to Employees

In today's complex and rapidly evolving workplace, emotional intelligence has emerged as a critical skill for employees aiming for professional excellence. Beyond the standard metrics of performance and technical expertise, EQ offers an added layer of capabilities that can be the distinguishing factor in career advancement, team collaboration, and overall job satisfaction. As we navigate through the intricacies of modern corporate dynamics, understanding the specific benefits of emotional intelligence becomes pivotal for both individual contributors and leaders. Here, we delve into how a well-developed EQ can significantly enhance various aspects of an employee's professional life while also enriching their personal experiences.

Helps Employees to Move to the Next Level

Emotional intelligence is not just about recognizing emotions but leveraging them for career advancement. It aids in self-awareness and self-management, helping employees make informed decisions and maintain composure in high-pressure situations. These skills pave the way for professional growth and leadership roles while also improving personal decision-making capabilities. By being more self-aware, you can identify the skills you need to improve, which can be useful in both your career and personal development plans. Good self-management skills can help you navigate personal challenges more effectively, from finances to relationships. These universally useful skills make emotional intelligence indispensable for holistic growth.

Teaches Employees How to React to Constructive Criticism

In the professional world, constructive criticism is a path to growth. High EQ means you perceive this feedback as an opportunity for improvement rather than a personal attack. This constructive mindset aids in professional development and personal growth, as you can apply the feedback to improve both work-related skills and personal habits. Learning to accept and utilize feedback in a work setting can translate into being more open to constructive comments in your personal relationships, thus fostering growth in both areas. Furthermore, this skill makes you more adaptable and agile, both as a professional and an individual, enabling you to face life's unpredictability with resilience.

Helps Employees Conquer Their Fears, Doubts, and Insecurities

Understanding and overcoming emotional barriers can aid in personal and professional development. By addressing the root causes of these fears, employees build greater self-confidence and dismantle limiting beliefs. This enhanced self-concept encourages them to take calculated risks, accept new challenges, and actualize their full potential both at work and in personal endeavors. Overcoming fears and insecurities can open the doors to new opportunities, be it a promotion at work or taking the leap into a new hobby or relationship. Moreover, the confidence gained through overcoming fears can make you a role model, inspiring both colleagues and loved ones to challenge their own limitations. The ability to strategize and confront fears is a universally applicable skill that will serve you well in all walks of life.

The Components of Emotional Intelligence

Emotional intelligence is a multidimensional competency comprising five core components: self-awareness, self-regulation, empathy, motivation, and social skills. While distinct, these facets work synergistically to endow individuals with the tools to excel across personal and professional domains. By developing each area, people can unlock their fullest potential and bring more wisdom, compassion, and success into their lives and organizations. This section will explore the key elements constituting emotional intelligence and how enhancing these skills translates into positive outcomes.

Self-Awareness

Self-awareness involves understanding one's own emotions, strengths, weaknesses, values, and goals. It provides the foundation for personal growth and development. By cultivating self-awareness, individuals can identify areas requiring improvement and play to their natural strengths when pursuing opportunities. This introspective capacity allows for ongoing self-evaluation and refinement. Enhancing self-awareness requires setting aside time for regular reflection through journaling, meditation, and open dialogues with trusted mentors. This inward focus gradually reveals blind spots, uncovers growth opportunities, and breeds self-actualization.

Cultivating self-awareness is like turning a spotlight inward. At first, you squint against the glare, unsure what you'll find in the shadows. But over time, your eyes adjust, allowing you to appreciate the intricate details that define you. The journey reveals unexplored passions, lingering fears, and forgotten dreams. You uncover who you were, who you are, and who you hope to become. With this understanding, you gain the power to rewrite limiting narratives, reinforce developing strengths, and chart an authentic path ahead. Self-awareness lights the way.

Self-Regulation

Self-regulation is the ability to manage emotions and impulses. It allows individuals to think before acting, adapt to changing circumstances, and persevere through challenges. Self-regulation promotes level-headedness and composure even in high-pressure situations. Individuals refrain from knee-jerk reactions, maintaining restraint and rationality. This skill empowers people to respond appropriately to feedback, constructive criticism, and trying scenarios. Techniques like deep breathing, TEMP listening, and cognitive reappraisal can be cultivated to enhance self-regulation. With practice, these become healthy default responses to stress.

Mastering self-regulation is akin to learning an instrument. At first, the scales are shaky, the notes discordant. But with routine practice, your dexterity improves. What once seemed impossible becomes fluid, even automatic. Self-regulation follows a similar trajectory—the skills strengthen through use. Tempering emotional reactions takes diligence; you must catch yourself in the heat of the moment. But the more you pause, process, and respond thoughtfully, the more natural it becomes. Your range expands; you play life's chaotic melodies with poise.

Empathy

Empathy means recognizing and understanding others' perspectives, feelings, and needs. It enables compassionate decision-making and conflict resolution. By seeing through the lens of another, individuals can tailor communications and actions to resonate appropriately. Empathy facilitates fruitful collaborations and reductions in misunderstandings. It is a keystone of healthy interpersonal relationships. Empathy can be strengthened by actively listening, asking thoughtful questions, and suspending one's own assumptions and judgments. This fosters mutual understanding and humanizes those around us.

Empathy blossoms when you water the seeds of human connection. Get curious about strangers; ask heartfelt questions. Listen with raw presence as their stories unfold. Suspend judgment as you step into their shoes. See the beauty that dwells beneath their flaws. Recognize the fears, hopes, and dreams that animate us all. Let empathy flourish, even when distrust seems wiser. Its roots run deep when planted in open soil. In time, you'll notice green shoots of understanding change everything they touch.

Motivation

Motivation pertains to one's drive, optimism, and passion. It empowers people to pursue meaningful goals with resilience. Motivation breeds enthusiasm, initiative, and commitment. Individuals high in motivation view obstacles as opportunities for growth. They operate with a solutions-focused mindset and a belief in their abilities. This mental toughness allows them to actualize their visions. Reframing setbacks, celebrating small wins, and nurturing passions are ways to boost motivation over the long term. This instills the grit and tenacity required for personal and professional excellence.

Motivation is the current that energizes our dreams. Some days the flow is weak; you must coax it along through trial and error. Celebrate when a spark catches; let it energize your purpose. On other days, inspiration strikes like lightning, jolting you with possibility. Channel this surge toward your goals. Motivation ebbs and flows, an endless cycle. During the lulls, reflect on how far you've come. When it crests, ride the wave ever forward. Stay centered through the rhythms; let commitment carry you. With patience and care, motivation becomes an unstoppable force.

Social Skills

Social skills allow individuals to communicate clearly, foster relationships, work in teams, and influence others positively. These competencies facilitate the building of rapport and negotiation of complex group dynamics. Social skills empower employees to become collaborative leaders who can provide constructive feedback, mediate conflict, and promote shared objectives. This ability to navigate interpersonal complexity allows organizations to harness diverse talents harmoniously. Social skills can be honed through public speaking training, volunteering, and proactive relationship-building across the company. With practice, socially intelligent behaviors become second nature.

Social skills are honed through practice, like training for a marathon. At first, the interpersonal terrain feels awkward and draining. But little by little, your endurance builds. You learn to pace yourself, listen intently, and project assured warmth. Your confidence grows with accomplished milestones. Before long, you're traversing complex group dynamics with ease. Yet, always hold a beginner's mind; there is nuance still to learn. Maintain humility, curiosity, and care. In relational fitness, the training never ends. But connection makes the journey profound.

The components of emotional intelligence work in concert to endow individuals with critical skills for navigating life's complexities. While innate temperament plays a role, dedicating time and effort toward developing each facet can yield profound rewards. As individuals level up their emotional intelligence, they gain the self-knowledge, discipline, wisdom, drive, and interpersonal awareness to thrive. Both individuals and organizations stand to benefit enormously from promoting multi-tiered emotional intelligence growth. By making it a priority, people can reach their highest potential and collectively elevate their communities.

Self-Assessment Exercises to Gauge Your Current EQ

Gauging one's current emotional intelligence allows for targeted growth and improvement. Through mindful self-evaluation, we can identify areas of strength to leverage as well as skills requiring further cultivation. Various reflective exercises provide valuable data points to enhance our self-awareness. While innate temperament differs, dedicating time to assess and develop your EQ skills will undoubtedly expand your capacity over time.

The EQ Balance Assessment

This exercise evaluates how balanced your EQ skills are across different contexts. For one week, track scenarios where you demonstrate self-awareness, self-regulation, empathy, motivation, and social skills on a scale of 1–5 (1 = poor, 5 = excellent). Calculate your average for each EQ component. A balanced score across categories indicates higher overall emotional intelligence. Make this a weekly practice to benchmark progress over time. Comparing assessments during periods of major stress versus calm can also reveal how challenged environments impact your EQ equilibrium. Strive for consistency.

The EQ Blind Spot Analysis

Have a trusted partner who knows you well complete an abbreviated EQ assessment on your behalf. Then, complete the same assessment about yourself and compare scores. Discrepancies reveal potential blind spots—EQ skills you may under or overestimate. Explore these further through journaling. Ask your partner follow-up questions about situations demonstrating your blind spots to gain deeper insight. Uncover if these align with past feedback you've resisted. Leverage this knowledge to expand self-awareness.

The EQ Stress Response Evaluation

Note your emotional responses, actions, and recovery times when facing stressors for two weeks. Does your EQ remain steady or fluctuate? Can you identify triggers tied to lower EI? Stronger self-regulation and faster rebound times correlate to higher emotional intelligence. Also reflect on any unhealthy coping mechanisms you turn to during stress. Do you isolate, overeat, or self-medicate? Work to replace these with healthy EI-building practices over time.

The EQ Conflict Resolution Analysis

Reflect on recent conflicts—professional and personal. Analyze your EQ skills demonstrated based on how conflicts arose, were addressed, and resolved. Did you remain calm? Empathize? Communicate effectively? Conflicts engaged through high EQ lead to constructive outcomes. Consider your internal self-talk during the conflict. Did you make negative assumptions? Revisit tough scenarios and reimagine more elevated responses. This strengthens EQ for future clashes.

The EQ Social Litmus Test

Ask trusted acquaintances to describe your top interpersonal strengths and weaknesses. Listen without judgment. Do their perceptions align with your self-assessment? Inconsistencies indicate areas of lower social self-awareness. Use feedback to improve social skills. Discuss positive and negative examples they recall that illuminate your social EQ in action. Uncover what responses elevated or escalated situations. Internalize insights.

Regular emotional intelligence check-ins empower us to become the best version of ourselves. However, the key is to approach assessments from a non-judgmental and growth-oriented mindset. View results as impartial data to inform positive change rather than as fixed evaluations of your worth. With consistent practice, you'll notice measurable improvements in self-awareness, self-regulation, empathy, motivation, and social skills. Celebrate progress made; allow insights to deepen your wisdom. Our emotional intelligence is continually evolving—let self-assessments illuminate the path ahead.

The Impact of EQ on Your Life

Emotional intelligence is not just an abstract concept—it profoundly shapes how we show up in all areas of life. By cultivating our EQ, we can unlock a breadth of tangible benefits in our relationships, careers, and personal growth. Understanding these multifaceted impacts provides motivation to continuously develop our emotional skills. This section will explore how optimized emotional intelligence facilitates both external success and inner fulfillment.

Personal Impacts

High emotional intelligence allows us to engage in healthy relationships built on empathy, vulnerability, and trust. Strong intrapersonal skills make us more aware of our needs and emotions. Interpersonal skills enable us to communicate lovingly, manage conflict constructively, and support our loved ones through challenges. We become steadier partners, parents, and friends. On an individual level, EI fosters inner peace, life satisfaction, and the resilience to navigate adversity. We understand our feelings, channel them productively, and fill our lives with meaning. By approaching relationships with authentic care, active listening, and selflessness, we build our circle of trust. Bonds deepen, and we find fulfillment in nurturing people's growth.

Professional Impacts

Emotionally intelligent employees excel in their careers. Intrapersonal skills like self-motivation and time management allow people to accomplish goals independently. Interpersonal aptitudes, including leadership, collaboration, and conflict resolution, facilitate team cohesion and workplace harmony. Together, these enable professional excellence. Emotionally intelligent individuals also cope effectively with job stress, adapt to changes, and act with integrity. Their composure, people skills, and positivity make them magnets for opportunity. Emotionally intelligent people identify their passions and align their career paths accordingly. They become invested employees who handle workplace relationships skillfully. Their ambition is tempered by wisdom and principle.

Impacts on Growth

On a personal growth trajectory, emotional intelligence is indispensable. Self-awareness provides the foundation for identifying areas requiring improvement; self-regulation gives us the discipline to change habits. Empathy develops compassion; motivation drives us forward. Socially, we learn to give and receive feedback productively. By leveraging these competencies, our emotional intelligence expands—unlocking our greatest potential. With higher EI, we have the self-knowledge to set ambitious goals, perseverance to overcome obstacles, and interpersonal awareness to learn from others. Our journey is amplified exponentially. Growth itself fortifies our emotional intelligence, fueling an upward spiral. We extract lessons from each challenge faced and connections made.

In many ways, emotional intelligence is the master key that opens the door to thriving across interwoven aspects of life. While technical skills may propel isolated domains of achievement, EI enables excellence holistically. Progress in one dimension fuels positive change across the board. Ultimately, a high level of emotional intelligence allows us to build healthy, happy lives of purpose and human connection. The journey brings out our best selves—someone wiser, more compassionate, and better equipped to leave a meaningful legacy. By recognizing EI's profoundly positive impacts, we can chart a course toward sustainable success.

Wrapping Up

In exploring the foundations of emotional intelligence, we've uncovered how this meta-ability acts as the cornerstone for fulfillment in life and work. Far more than a passing fad, EI represents a paradigm shift—one that illuminates the critical skills we must cultivate to thrive in an increasingly complex world.

In this chapter, we

- defined emotional intelligence and its components.
- discussed the benefits of EI across personal, professional, and growth domains.
- explored assessments to gauge current EI levels.
- recognized EI's profound impacts on relationships, careers, and self-actualization.

Armed with this knowledge, we can begin leveling up our own emotional intelligence. As we've learned, self-awareness represents the first step in this journey. In the next chapter, we'll explore core practices to enhance self-awareness—spotlighting our inner world so we can navigate life's challenges with greater wisdom and grace. Deepening self-knowledge lights the path ahead.

Case Study: Sarah

Imagine Sarah, a manager at a bustling tech firm. She was competent, diligent, and fiercely committed to her job. But even with all these qualities, she sensed an undercurrent of tension rippling through her team. Things were just not clicking. Puzzled and frustrated, she stumbled upon the concept known as emotional intelligence, or EQ, and it was as if the universe itself sent her a guidebook.

Sarah didn't just skim through the concept; she dove deep. She was hungry for transformation, so she started by looking inward—self-awareness. She asked for 360-degree feedback, not just from her higher-ups but from her team members as well. And let me tell you, she was open enough to listen. The feedback wasn't all roses and sunshine, but it offered her the raw, gritty gift of perspective. She now had a roadmap drawn by others, but for her.

Moving on to self-regulation, she started practicing mindfulness. Who among us hasn't shot off an email in a moment of frustration and regretted it minutes later? Sarah became a master of the pause, giving herself the space to choose her reactions rather than being held hostage by them. The impact this had on her team was like a ripple in a pond—calmness started spreading, and stress levels dipped.

Then came the cornerstone of human connection: empathy. Sarah scheduled one-on-one chats with every single team member. Not to critique or strategize, but to listen, to truly hear the stories each person brought to the table. She replaced judgment with curiosity. The result? Her team started to feel seen, maybe for the first time in their professional lives. They felt safe and valued, and that changed the entire vibe of the workspace.

Motivated to build on this momentum, Sarah took a fresh look at her team's goals. She tailored them to play to each individual's strengths and dovetailed them with their unique aspirations. And this wasn't just managerial flair; this was leadership that was emotionally intelligent, leading from the heart and the head. The team wasn't just clocking in hours now; they were engaged, motivated, and fully showing up.

Lastly, the social maestro that she was becoming, Sarah fostered an environment of genuine teamwork and communication. She built in time for team-building exercises that weren't just about falling back and trusting someone to catch you, but about leaning into difficult conversations, navigating conflict, and coming out stronger together.

In less than a year, this embrace of EQ transformed not just Sarah, but her entire team. Productivity surged by 30%, and staff turnover plunged. She earned the accolade of "Most Improved Leader of the Year," but more than that, she earned the trust and respect of her team. She went to bed each night not just tired, but fulfilled.

Case Study: Mark

Mark's deepening understanding of emotional intelligence didn't just stop at identifying his areas for growth; it was as if he had been given a new lens through which to view the world. Previously, his interactions had been filled with hurried judgments and assumptions, a rush to get to the next thing, and a focus on his own immediate reactions. But once he grasped the importance of each component of emotional intelligence, he started slowing down and examining his thoughts and feelings more closely.

His improved self-awareness allowed him to recognize not just his own emotions but also how they influenced his behavior. The chapter explained that self-awareness was the cornerstone of emotional intelligence. Mark began journaling to track his emotions and their triggers, which became an eye-opening experience for him. He could now preempt feelings of irritation or anger and choose a more constructive response.

Self-regulation, his previously identified weak link, gradually began to strengthen as Mark applied different techniques. He used mindfulness exercises to stay present and focused, which had an unexpected but wonderful benefit—his stress levels started to plummet. He could handle disagreements better, not letting them escalate into full-blown conflicts. Even his friends began to notice how much calmer and more composed he had become in stressful situations.

Empathy was another area in which Mark felt he had room to grow. With a renewed perspective, he started putting himself in others' shoes more often. This made him a more compassionate friend and sibling. Now, when someone shared a concern or problem with him, he took the time to really listen and understand their point of view instead of hastily offering advice. This emotional generosity wasn't lost on his loved ones, who found their conversations with Mark to be increasingly meaningful and nourishing.

Motivation was another aspect of emotional intelligence that the chapter emphasized. Although Mark had always been reasonably driven, understanding the emotional aspects of motivation gave him an energy boost. He set personal goals that went beyond the superficial and found that striving for these deeper objectives made the journey more enjoyable.

His enhanced social skills were the cherry on top. Mark found himself better able to read the room, so to speak, and adapt his behavior accordingly. Whether he was at a casual gathering or a family dinner, he could sense the emotional currents and navigate them more adeptly.

And so, the cycle continued. The more Mark invested in his emotional intelligence, the richer his life became. His relationships thrived, his mental state stabilized, and his overall sense of well-being soared. He had tapped into a kind of emotional eloquence that allowed him to express himself fully and connect with others on a deeper level.

Mark's journey isn't unique; it's a journey open to anyone willing to delve into understanding and enhancing their emotional intelligence. The first step, as Mark discovered, is awareness, and from that foundation, an entirely new way of living and relating to others can flourish. Mark is a living testament to the untapped potential within us all, waiting just beneath the surface, ready to enrich our lives in ways we can't even imagine.

TWO

Step #2—Developing Self Awareness

> *We are dangerous when we are not conscious of our responsibility for how we behave, think, and feel.*
>
> Marshall B. Rosenberg

It's a powerful thought, isn't it? Rosenberg's words highlight a simple truth: When we're out of touch with our own emotions and motivations, things can quickly go awry. Think about it. How many times have misunderstandings or mistakes happened because we weren't fully tuned into our own feelings or those of others?

This chapter will break down the ins and outs of self-awareness. You'll learn why it's so vital, especially as a foundation of emotional intelligence. And by the time you finish this section, you won't just know what self-awareness is; you'll have tangible ways to grow and maintain it in your everyday life.

What Is Self-Awareness?

At its core, self-awareness is the conscious knowledge and understanding of one's own character, emotions, desires, and motivations. It's the process of reflecting on oneself, understanding personal strengths, weaknesses, and the impact one's actions can have on others. It involves both internal self-awareness—recognizing our own values, passions, and reactions—and external self-awareness—understanding how others perceive us. In essence, it's the ability to see ourselves clearly and objectively through introspection and reflection (Betz, 2022)

How Self-Awareness Helps With Emotional Intelligence

Self-awareness acts as the foundational pillar of emotional intelligence. It's the ability to understand your emotions, recognize their origins, and see their impact on your work and relationships. With solid self-awareness, individuals can more effectively harness their emotions, guiding them in productive directions rather than being controlled by them. By understanding oneself, it becomes easier to empathize with others, communicate effectively, and manage complex social situations. It's the starting point, and from there, other aspects of emotional intelligence—like self-regulation, motivation, and social skills—can be built upon and refined. Essentially, without a keen sense of self-awareness, true emotional intelligence is out of reach (Eurich, 2008).

Benefits of Being Self-Aware

Understanding oneself goes beyond introspection—it's about making active, informed changes in our lives. It's the lens through which we view our actions, reactions, and interactions. From the decisions we make in solitude to the choices we make amidst a crowd, self-awareness is pivotal. So, let's take a closer look at how self-awareness can reframe and redefine our experiences.

Better Management and Regulation of Emotions

When we're deeply in tune with our emotional world, it becomes second nature to manage and modulate our reactions. This doesn't mean suppressing emotions, but rather understanding them to channel them effectively. Such proactive emotional management can result in fewer moments of regret, lessened anxiety, and an overall feeling of control in life's unpredictable tide.

Improved Communication

Clear, concise communication starts with understanding oneself. When we know where we stand, it's easier to stand firm in conversations and to extend a hand in understanding. The ripple effects of this can be seen in daily interactions, leading to fewer conflicts, clearer expressions, and an overall smoother flow of thoughts and feelings.

Enhanced Decision-Making Skills

Decisions grounded in self-awareness are often those we look back on with confidence. We move forward not with uncertainty, but with a clarity that comes from a deep understanding of ourselves. It's this internal compass, shaped by self-awareness, that guides us through the fog of choices, helping us navigate with assurance.

Strengthened Relationships

The beauty of self-awareness is that while it starts with the self, it benefits everyone around us. Understanding oneself sets the stage for understanding others, leading to deeper, more meaningful connections. It's like building a bridge; the stronger the foundation, the more resilient and enduring the structure.

Higher Levels of Happiness

There's a unique contentment that comes from living a life aligned with our core beliefs. Each day feels less like going through the motions and more like a genuine expression of oneself. Over time, this continuous alignment paves the way for a lasting, deep-seated happiness that isn't easily shaken by external factors.

Increased Confidence

Confidence, in many ways, is a byproduct of understanding and accepting oneself—warts and all. Recognizing our strengths just as clearly as our areas for growth makes us more resilient in the face of adversity. Every setback becomes a lesson, every success a validation of our journey, all stemming from a deep root of self-awareness.

Elevated Job Satisfaction

Job satisfaction isn't just about the role we play but also about how that role resonates with our personal values. When the two align, work becomes less of a chore and more of a passion. The days become purpose-driven, challenges turn into opportunities, and the workspace evolves into an arena of growth and fulfillment.

Superior Leadership Skills

Effective leadership is as much about understanding oneself as it is about understanding one's team. A leader who is self-aware can tap into team dynamics in a nuanced way, fostering an environment of trust and mutual respect. It's this blend of personal insight and outward understanding that shapes leaders who are not only respected but also revered.

Self-awareness might seem like a personal endeavor, but its impact is profoundly universal. From shaping our individual journeys to influencing those around us, its reach is both deep and wide. It's not just about knowing oneself but about leveraging that knowledge to craft a life of meaning, purpose, and impact.

Techniques to Enhance Self-Awareness

Developing self-awareness is a lifelong endeavor, but the effort put into understanding oneself can yield powerful insights and growth. By nurturing this skill, we pave the way for more intentional living, improved relationships, and greater clarity in decision-making. Here's a deeper dive into ten techniques that can significantly boost self-awareness:

- **Keep an open mind:** Adopting an open-minded approach allows us to absorb diverse viewpoints and experiences. This acceptance can enrich our perspective and lead to more informed decisions. In a rapidly changing world, an open mind can be our best asset, ensuring adaptability and understanding (Cherry, 2023).
- **Be mindful of your strengths and weaknesses:** A well-rounded self-awareness requires acknowledgment of both strengths and areas of improvement. Celebrating our strengths boosts confidence while understanding our weaknesses provides opportunities for growth. Such balance fosters resilience, adaptability, and a genuine drive for self-improvement (Goleman, 2021).
- **Stay focused:** With so many distractions around, maintaining focus is essential for introspection. By dedicating time to reflect on our goals, values, and actions, we can uncover patterns and behaviors that define us. This dedicated reflection, free from distractions, acts as a mirror, revealing our true selves and guiding our future actions (Wallbridge, 2023).

- **Set boundaries:** Establishing boundaries is vital for mental and emotional well-being. It helps delineate our personal space, ensuring we don't spread ourselves too thin. With clear boundaries, we safeguard our energy, prioritize our well-being, and gain clarity about our needs and limits (Eurich, 2018).

- **Know your emotional triggers:** Recognizing our emotional triggers is the first step toward proactive emotional management. By identifying these triggers, we can preemptively strategize and avoid reactive behaviors. Understanding these emotional catalysts provides a level of control, enabling more rational responses even in heated situations (Eurich, 2018).

- **Embrace your intuition:** Intuition, often dubbed our "gut feeling," can offer insights that rational thought might miss. Trusting this instinctual knowledge can guide us in situations where data is limited or unclear. Cultivating and heeding our intuition adds another dimension to our decision-making arsenal, often leading to more holistic choices (Eurich, 2018).

- **Practice self-discipline:** Self-discipline shapes our actions and decisions, ensuring they align with our core values. By exercising control over impulses and making deliberate choices, we affirm our commitment to our goals. This commitment, coupled with regular reflection, fosters genuine growth and personal development (Wallbridge, 2023.).

- **Consider how your actions affect others:** Understanding the broader impact of our actions promotes empathy and community-mindedness. It's a reminder that we're part of an interconnected web and that our choices ripple beyond our immediate surroundings. This broader view nurtures compassionate choices and fosters deeper, more understanding relationships (Wallbridge, 2023).

- **Seek feedback:** Gathering feedback offers a window into how others perceive us. While self-reflection is vital, external perspectives can reveal blind spots and areas of growth. Embracing this feedback, especially from trusted sources, can lead to a richer, more well-rounded self-awareness (Eurich, 2018).

- **Engage in continuous learning:** Self-awareness is not a stagnant skill; it evolves with time and experience. Seeking new knowledge, experiences, and perspectives ensures our self-understanding remains current and relevant. As we continue to learn and grow, our self-awareness deepens, making the journey even more rewarding (Betz, 2022).

As we navigate the complexities of life, self-awareness emerges as a guiding light, illuminating our path and choices. By adopting and integrating these techniques, we commit to a life of intentionality, empathy, and genuine growth. It's a commitment that promises not only personal rewards but also a positive impact on the world around us.

Identifying Your Emotional Triggers

Emotions play a pivotal role in our daily interactions and experiences. While they can elevate our joys and deepen our connections, they can also sometimes take us by surprise, often due to specific triggers. Identifying these triggers is essential in managing our emotional responses and fostering a deeper understanding of ourselves.

What Is an Emotional Trigger?

An emotional trigger, often referred to as a mental trigger, is any topic, event, or situation that consistently evokes a strong emotional response, whether it's sadness, anger, or anxiety. It might not always align with what the majority would perceive as a standard response to the given stimulus. For instance, while one person might find joy in a particular song due to a positive memory associated with it, another person might find it saddening because it reminds them of a challenging time in their life. It's these personalized, often deep-seated connections that bring about intense emotional reactions (Miller, 2020).

Steps to Identifying an Emotional Trigger

- **Stay attuned to your feelings:** The first step is recognizing when you have a stronger emotional reaction than expected. Pay close attention to sudden feelings of discomfort, anger, sadness, or anxiety. These emotions are indicators that you've encountered a trigger.
- **Reflect on the cause:** Once you recognize the emotion, try to understand the root cause. What was happening when you felt that surge of emotion? Was it a comment someone made, a place, or maybe an anniversary of an event? Dig deep and try to connect the dots between the stimulus and your emotional response.
- **Keep a journal:** Documenting instances when you feel triggered can be enlightening. Over time, patterns might emerge, revealing specific triggers. This written record not only helps in identification but also in devising strategies to manage or avoid certain triggers.
- **Seek feedback:** Sometimes, an external perspective can offer invaluable insights. Talk to someone you trust about

your reactions. They might have observed patterns or triggers that you haven't noticed.

- **Practice mindfulness:** Engaging in mindfulness exercises can heighten your self-awareness. It allows you to be present, making it easier to spot triggers as they occur. This immediate recognition can often reduce the intensity of the emotional response.

Understanding and identifying our emotional triggers is a significant step toward self-awareness and emotional intelligence. By being proactive in this journey, we equip ourselves with tools to navigate the complexities of our emotional landscape, ensuring our reactions are both understood and manageable.

Journaling Exercises for Self-Reflection

Unearthing the deeper layers of our mind requires introspection, and what better way to dive into this than through journaling? Journaling helps us pause, reflect, and gain insight into our emotions, dreams, and aspirations. Remember, journaling can look different for everyone. To help you embark on this transformative journey, here are a series of exercises:

- **Gratitude list:** Kickstart your mornings by jotting down the everyday joys you encounter. This simple act can help shift your focus toward the positives, grounding you in a mindset of appreciation.
- **Envision the future:** Where do you see yourself a few years from now? Describe that place, those emotions, and the path you'd take to get there. Periodically revisiting this vision can help steer your present actions.

- **Past reflection:** Revisit the turning points in your life. How did those events shape you? Recognizing the lessons from our past can guide our future steps.
- **Current feelings:** Dive into your present emotions. What's bubbling beneath the surface today? By understanding our current state of mind, we can navigate our day more consciously.
- **Self-compassion letter:** We often need reminders of our worth. Write an uplifting letter to yourself, highlighting your strengths and offering gentle encouragement.
- **Life's highs and lows:** Plot out the emotional journey of your past month or year. What events or moments stood out? Reflecting on these can provide a balanced perspective on life's roller coaster.
- **Describe your ideal day:** Paint a picture of a perfect day from dawn to dusk. What would it entail? By dreaming about our ideal scenarios, we get a clearer sense of our desires and values.
- **Conversations with your future self:** Engage in a dialogue with the person you aspire to be. What wisdom would this future self share? Such an exercise can offer a fresh perspective on present challenges.
- **Personal values:** Pen down the core values that guide your decisions. How did they influence your recent choices? Revisiting these values ensures our actions are consistently aligned with our beliefs.
- **Face your fears:** Confront the shadows lurking in your mind. Describe them, dissect them, and challenge them. Addressing our fears head-on can diminish their hold on us.
- **Personal achievements:** List out your proud moments, however big or small. How did they make you feel?

Celebrating our victories instills confidence and
motivation.

- **Dream analysis:** Recall a recent dream and dissect its
  themes and emotions. Dreams can offer unexpected
  insights into our subconscious, shedding light on
  suppressed feelings or desires.

Committing to the practice of journaling invites clarity and
growth. With each written word, we gain a deeper understanding
of our inner world, helping us shape a life that resonates with our
true selves.

The Mirror Exercise: Seeing Yourself Through Another's Eyes

One insightful technique for building self-awareness is what I call
the "mirror exercise." This involves envisioning yourself from
another person's perspective and considering how they might
describe you. The goal is to step outside your own biases and see
yourself through an objective lens. Here are some steps for this
reflective practice:

- **Choose your "mirror."** This could be a close friend, family
  member, colleague, or even a stranger who has observed
  you. Select someone who can provide an honest,
  thoughtful perspective on how you come across.
- **Imagine seeing yourself through their eyes.** Try to set
  aside your own judgments and self-perceptions. Adopt
  their vantage point and consider how they might describe
  your personality, habits, speech patterns, body language,
  and other tendencies.
- **Note your observations.** Jot down descriptive words and
  phrases they might use. Don't filter or edit the descriptions

—the goal is raw objectivity. Pay attention to both positive and critical observations.

- **Look for alignment and disconnects.** Compare their imagined narrative to your self-perceptions. Are there overlaps or contradictions? What insights emerge from seeing yourself mirrored back in this way?
- **Ask for actual feedback.** To gain an added layer of insight, you could ask your chosen "mirror" for feedback on how they actually perceive you. Compare their real impressions to the ones you imagined.
- **Integrate new perspectives.** Use any eye-opening observations to build greater self-understanding. Look for ways to retain beneficial qualities and evolve areas that need work.

Regularly practicing this exercise with different "mirrors" provides invaluable external perspectives we often overlook. It sheds light on our blind spots and gives a well-rounded view of how the world sees us. Over time, these objective insights help us grow into our best and most self-aware selves.

Exploring Your Core Values Through Reflection

Our values serve as an inner compass, guiding our choices and behaviors. But in the rush of daily life, they often fade into the background. Intentionally identifying and reflecting on your core values provides clarity and focus. Here are some useful exercises:

- Review your recent decisions—what values influenced them? Look for recurring themes to reveal your priorities.
- Imagine your 80th birthday party—what would you want people to describe as your values?

- Write your ideal obituary and consider what values you'd want highlighted.
- Make two lists—moments when you felt happiest and most distressed. What values were present or missing?
- If you could instill one value in your children, what would it be? Why?
- What qualities do you admire most in your role models or heroes? Do you embody those values?
- When have you compromised your values? How did it impact you? What values were neglected?
- Which daily activities align with your values? Which feel disconnected?
- If you could have a billboard anywhere, what value would you promote on it?
- What principles guide your friendships and relationships?

Regular value reflection provides a compass when you feel adrift and clarity when faced with difficult choices. It's an empowering practice for gaining self-awareness.

Cultivating Self-Compassion

In our quest for self-awareness, we must not only understand our strengths and weaknesses—but embrace them with compassion. Self-compassion entails treating ourselves with care, concern, and understanding—especially during difficult times. When integrated as part of self-awareness, it provides:

- A buffer against self-criticism and negative self-talk. With self-compassion, we counterbalance constructive self-reflection with kindness.

- Greater emotional resilience. Self-compassion helps us cope with challenging emotions, failures, and setbacks with wisdom and grace.
- Deeper self-motivation. We avoid destructive perfectionism and speak to ourselves as we would a close friend—with encouragement.
- Healthier boundaries. Self-compassion teaches us to say no when needed and prioritize our well-being.
- Enhanced self-care. We make self-compassion actionable through soothing activities like meditation, yoga, and journaling.
- More courage to be vulnerable. By embracing our imperfections, we open ourselves to authentic human connection.
- Increased empathy. Accepting our own flaws allows for a deeper understanding of others.

Practical Tips for Self-Compassion:

- Notice self-judgmental thoughts and consciously reframe them with gentleness.
- Treat yourself with the caring actions and words you would show a friend in need.
- Recall a time you felt comforted and channel that feeling toward yourself.
- Write a heartfelt letter to yourself expressing understanding for your flaws.
- Imagine yourself as a child and provide the care your inner child needs.
- Ask: Would I say this to someone I love? If not, don't say it to yourself.
- See failures as opportunities for growth, not condemnation.

• Surround yourself with those who reinforce your intrinsic self-worth.

With its ethos of wisdom and care for oneself, self-compassion provides the nourishing soil for self-awareness to take root and blossom into its fullest, most beautiful expression.

The Art of Receiving Feedback

Our blind spots obscure what is clear to others. Feedback offers an invaluable external mirror into our impact and behaviors. But beyond simply receiving feedback, we must learn to accept it gracefully and integrate it constructively. Here are some best practices:

- **Listen openly:** Avoid knee-jerk defensiveness. Create a safe space for the feedback giver to speak honestly and be fully heard. Offer your complete presence.
- **Ask reflective questions:** Seek to understand their perspective fully. Ask for specific examples or clarification. Inquire about the feelings evoked or needs being unmet.
- **Express appreciation:** Thank them for caring enough and risking discomfort to share this gift of insight with you. Appreciate their courage.
- **Consider carefully:** Reflect deeply on the feedback over time. What core truth rings clear? How can this elevate your self-awareness?
- **Integrate selectively:** Not all feedback warrants change. Consider the source and their motive. Determine what rings true. Let the rest go.
- **Enact mindfully:** If the feedback reveals a blind spot needing attention, brainstorm small mindful steps. Don't try changing everything overnight.

- **Circle back:** Once you've had time to integrate, follow up with the giver. Share your appreciation again, along with your game plan for growth.

This form of receptive, discerning openness to feedback cultivates self-awareness. Our critics can become our teachers when we develop the courage to listen, reflect, and grow.

Wrapping Up

Looking back to the insight from Marshall B. Rosenberg about the responsibility tied to our actions and feelings, it's evident just how pivotal self-awareness is in our lives. This expanded chapter has provided additional tools and understanding to navigate your emotional terrain with greater confidence.

We've now covered the following:

- a deep dive into what self-awareness truly means and why it's crucial
- the wide-ranging benefits that come from being in tune with oneself
- practical steps and reflective exercises to enrich your self-awareness
- ways to receive feedback and cultivate self-compassion on the journey

With this strengthened foundation of self-understanding, we can craft lives of deeper purpose, wisdom, and compassion. As we turn the page, we'll carry these lessons forward, exploring the intricacies of resilience and how self-awareness equips us to thrive.

Case Study: Jack

Meet Jack. He was a middle school teacher in a small suburban community. His work was demanding, both emotionally and intellectually. He was the kind of teacher who wouldn't just teach algebra but would also delve into the emotional lives of his students. Yet, despite his best intentions, his classroom dynamics were shaky. Why? Jack himself couldn't put a finger on it. Until he decided that the place to start wasn't with his students; it was with himself. The realm of self-awareness.

With courage as his compass, Jack started exploring what self-awareness actually meant. It wasn't a self-indulgent navel-gazing exercise but a multidimensional lens through which he learned to see his thoughts, emotions, and actions. He started with introspection but extended it to be receptive to feedback, even when it was tough to hear. The multiple facets of his character started revealing themselves, and he realized that self-awareness was not just knowing himself but also understanding how he was perceived by others. It was like a song; it wasn't enough to just know the lyrics; you needed to hear how it sounded to others.

Jack became aware of his emotional patterns, the triggers that took him off course. He started recognizing that his irritability wasn't because his students were challenging but because he was stressed about aging parents, a mortgage, and life's other curveballs. With this newfound awareness, he found he was better able to manage his reactions, his communication sharpened, and his relationships deepened. His students began to trust him more, and even his personal relationships bloomed. Self-awareness had made him a happier person, a more fulfilled teacher, and a more supportive friend and family member.

Committed to staying on this transformative path, Jack deployed a range of techniques to hone his self-awareness. He started journaling, capturing his thoughts, feelings, and a-ha moments. He practiced mindfulness, observing his thoughts without judgment. He even learned to set boundaries, recognizing that self-care wasn't selfish but essential for balanced living. One of his most transformative practices was identifying his emotional triggers. For Jack, it was the sense of not being heard, stemming from his childhood. Recognizing this allowed him to navigate emotional landscapes—both his and others—with far greater ease.

Journaling became Jack's go-to tool for reflection. He scribbled down his worries, his aspirations, and even his daily mundane interactions. And every time he did, he found a piece of himself in those ink marks. It was like each entry brought clarity, like wiping a foggy windowpane until he could see clearly. As he journaled, he understood himself better and, in doing so, understood his students, friends, and loved ones more deeply. too.

So, circling back to where we began, the lack of self-awareness wasn't just a personal deficit; it was a relational one. The responsibility for how we behaved, thought, and felt didn't just impact us; it rippled into every life we touched. And just like Jack, it was this awakening that not only helped us live authentically but elevated our very humanness. You weren't just gaining insight into how you ticked, but you were also acquiring the ability to engage with the world in a way that was transformative.

Case Study: Sam

You know, it's funny how life has a way of pushing us to make changes, right? Take Sam, for example, a 35-year-old guy who'd been feeling like something was missing for years. He wasn't unhappy, per se, but he often felt disconnected—from his job, from his friends, and even from Tracy, his long-time partner.

One evening, he and Tracy had one of those arguments— you know, the kind that makes you stop and question things. The kind that makes you think, *How did we get here?* It was in that moment of reflection that he stumbled upon a book about emotional intelligence and got curious about this thing called self-awareness. Like, what does that even mean?

So, Sam figured he'd give it a go. He bought a journal—nothing fancy, just a notebook—and started jotting down what he felt each day, what ticked him off, what made him happy, all that good stuff. It didn't take long before he noticed a pattern. Work stress was his kryptonite. If he had a bad day at the office, you bet it would spill into his home life.

Realizing that was a game-changer, he thought, *I've got to handle this stress thing better.* That's when he took up mindfulness. Now, this isn't some mystical thing; he simply started taking short breaks to breathe, clear his head, that sort of thing. He even signed up for a meditation class.

And you won't believe the ripple effect this had. At work, Sam found he was making better choices. He was like a stress detective, catching himself before stress could muddle his thinking. He even noticed he was getting along better with his colleagues. Who would've thought?

But here's the real kicker: his relationship with Tracy? Night and day difference. They still had their disagreements—hey, who doesn't?—but now, Sam was a lot better at saying what was actually bothering him. No more shouting matches: they'd sit, talk, and most of the time, figure things out.

He started feeling better about pretty much everything. His days felt purposeful, and he was genuinely happier. It's as if the fog lifted and he could see the world more clearly. The best part? He knew exactly what was important to him, and that made it easier to invest time in the things—and people—that really mattered.

A year into this whole self-discovery adventure, Sam couldn't believe the change. It wasn't just about understanding himself better; it was like he had this toolset for dealing with life's ups and downs. So, yeah, Sam's story is one of those real-life testimonies to how making a commitment to understanding yourself can seriously upgrade your life—be it your job, your relationships, or just your own peace of mind.

THREE

Step #3—Building Emotional Resilience

 We cannot tell what may happen to us in the strange medley of life. But we can decide what happens in us — how we can take it, what we do with it — and that is what really counts in the end.

Joseph Fort Newton

This insightful quote perfectly captures the spirit of what this chapter is all about. Life's curveballs are inevitable, but our reactions to them are entirely up to us. So, how do we ensure that our internal responses are as constructive as possible? That's where emotional resilience comes into play. With this skill in your toolbox, you're not just weathering life's storms; you're learning how to dance in the rain.

Welcome to Chapter 3, where we're tackling the robust subject of emotional resilience head-on. Think of this skill as your personal shield against life's trials and tribulations. The core idea here is not just about "making it through" but truly flourishing no matter what comes your way. The aim? To unlock your ability to bounce back from adversity effortlessly and with newfound wisdom.

The focus of this chapter goes beyond mere survival. It's about prospering. Whether you're navigating office politics, juggling personal responsibilities, or dealing with downright tough times, resilience equips you to face these challenges, grow from them, and come out the other side stronger than ever.

Understanding Emotional Resilience

You might hear this term and think it's some sort of emotional superhero cape we can throw on to dodge life's bullets. But it's not about that, not at all. Emotional resilience is less about dodging and more about showing up in your life, challenges and all.

Consider the experience of losing a client at work. It's easy to plunge into a whirlpool of self-doubt and negativity. But if you're practicing emotional resilience, you acknowledge the pain without getting consumed by it. You say to yourself, "This hurts, but what can I learn from it? How can I evolve?" You're not shoving emotions aside; you're looking them in the eye and asking them what they have to teach you.

Or imagine you've just gone through a gut-wrenching breakup. Emotional resilience doesn't mean plastering a fake smile on your face and declaring you're fine. No. It means allowing yourself to feel the ache in your heart while also knowing this is a chapter, not your entire book. It means asking yourself, "How can I heal in a way that respects my feelings but also leads me to growth?" You lean into the discomfort just enough to come out stronger on the other end.

And let's be clear: This isn't just motivational fluff. Emotional resilience is grounded in a rich bedrock of research (Fritz et al.,

2018) that touches on emotional well-being, mental health, and general life satisfaction. It's the real deal.

So, here's the bottom line: Emotional resilience is not about skating over life's challenges or denying your emotions. It's about fully engaging with your life—messy parts and all—and making conscious choices about how you respond to adversity. It's not about becoming emotion-proof; it's about becoming emotion-wise.

Benefits of Emotional Resilience

What do you get out of emotional resilience? Because, let's face it, if you're going to invest your heart and soul into developing this skill, you want to know it's worth it. And let me tell you, the benefits are manifold and they hit you right where you live: in your relationships, your workplace, and deep inside that beautiful mess we call the human psyche.

First up, emotional resilience is your golden ticket to better mental health. We're talking less anxiety, less depression, and a real boost to your general mood. When life tries to knock you down, emotional resilience helps you get back up with your dignity intact. And the cool part? The stronger your emotional resilience, the less likely you are to get knocked down in the first place.

Now, let's talk about relationships—arguably the meat and potatoes of life. Emotional resilience helps you cultivate deeper, more authentic connections. It's like you have this emotional toolkit, and when misunderstandings or conflicts arise, instead of throwing your hands up, you're like, "I got this." You dig into that toolkit and pull out empathy, active listening, and constructive communication. So, instead of driving people away, you're drawing them closer.

And what about your professional life? Imagine walking into a high-stakes meeting or negotiation. With emotional resilience, you're not a ball of stress; you're centered. Even if the conversation goes south, you maintain your poise and navigate through the storm without losing sight of your goals. You're not just surviving your workday; you're owning it.

Here's another nugget of truth: Emotional resilience even plays into your physical well-being. Yes, you heard me right. Stress takes a toll on the body, but resilience acts like a shield. It's associated with lower rates of illness and quicker recovery times. Your body and mind are intrinsically linked, and emotional resilience nurtures that connection.

And you don't have to take my word for it. A wealth of research supports these benefits, from improved mental well-being to enhanced relationship quality and even better physical health. Science backs this up as solidly as a sturdy oak tree.

Emotional resilience is not some abstract, nice-to-have quality. It's a game-changer. It's what equips you to live your life fully, with a heart wide open to both joys and challenges. And let me tell you, living life in full color like that is something you don't want to miss.

Strategies for Coping With Stress and Adversity

The reality of life is that we all encounter hardships, obstacles, and stressors. This is where good coping skills become invaluable. They serve as a protective shield, enabling us to manage life's challenges with resilience and composure. These coping abilities don't just save us from emotional turbulence; they also have profound implications for our physical well-being, guarding against stress-induced health problems. With coping skills at your disposal, you gain the mental clarity and focus required to function optimally in your personal and professional life.

How to Cope With Stress and Adversity

To understand the true essence of coping, it's important to start with self-awareness. Recognizing when you're stressed isn't as simple as it sounds. Whether it manifests as physical sensations like a racing heart or emotional states like feeling overwhelmed, the key is to identify these stress signals early on. Once you do, techniques like deep breathing or even taking a brief walk can alter your emotional landscape.

Another cornerstone of effective coping involves shifting your perspective. During a crisis, it's easy to blow things out of proportion. A moment of pause to ask yourself, "Will this matter in a year? Or in five years?" can drastically alter your emotional response and help you keep the larger picture in view.

Don't underestimate the role of social support, either. A meaningful conversation with a trusted friend or family member can provide not just emotional relief, but often insights and solutions as well. Sometimes, sharing your burden can make it feel lighter.

But what about those times when facing the issue head-on feels too intense? It's completely all right to distract yourself briefly. Healthy distractions like reading, a warm bath, or watching a favorite TV show can be like emotional pit stops, giving you the energy to face your challenges afresh.

Then, there's the empowering act of problem-solving. Instead of dwelling on the problem, direct your mental energy toward devising practical solutions. You can start by breaking down the problem into smaller tasks and addressing them individually. This proactive approach can give you a sense of control, even when circumstances seem uncontrollable.

It's also crucial to challenge and reassess your thoughts. Cognitive reappraisal, where you consciously alter your interpretation of stressful situations, can be remarkably effective. You can train yourself to reframe your thoughts in a way that reduces emotional distress.

Finally, there's no shame in seeking professional help. Sometimes, our own coping strategies fall short, and that's when the guidance of a qualified expert can make a world of difference.

So, in essence, learning to cope is a continuous process. As you improve your coping skills, you'll find you're not just surviving, but thriving—living a life that is as fulfilling as it is resilient.

Understanding the Connection Between Emotional Intelligence and Growth Mindset

If we look at emotional intelligence and growth mindset as two friends sitting in a coffee shop, deep in meaningful conversation, we'll see how intertwined they really are. Emotional intelligence is that friend who truly listens, not just to us but to everyone around them. It's the friend who helps us recognize and name our feelings. With emotional intelligence, we're not just responding to life; we're really living it, feeling our way through it. This sets the stage for its coffee shop companion—a growth mindset. A growth mindset is our friend who nudges us to see every stumble as a setup for a leap. Together, they're a pair that inspires us to see challenges as chances, not just trials to endure but opportunities to soar.

Growth Mindset vs. Fixed Mindset

When we think of mindsets, we often place them into two boxes: fixed and growth. A fixed mindset whispers that our talents and capabilities are pre-determined. It's like saying, "This is the hand you're dealt. Deal with it." It's a storyline that many of us know too well. But there's another narrative, one of expansion and possibilities—that's a growth mindset. This mindset isn't just about proving how smart or talented we are; it's about stretching, evolving, and discovering what we're capable of. You know, the delicious realization that we're more elastic than static.

Benefits of a Growth Mindset

Ever think about what's in it for you when you start looking at life through the lens of a growth mindset? Besides the obvious benefits like becoming a more adaptable and engaging human being? A growth mindset doesn't just make you resilient; it makes you alive to change, less defensive, and more open. It's like having a sturdy yet supple backbone that supports you as you take risks and explore the unknown. You become not just the student but also the teacher, and your world grows larger. The ripple effect touches your relationships and your work, enriching them in ways that you might not have expected but will definitely appreciate.

Strategies for Developing a Growth Mindset

So, how do you foster this mindset that champions growth? It starts by understanding that challenges are less about confronting roadblocks and more about welcoming signposts. These signposts guide you toward personal development, not divert you from it. Embracing a sense of persistence is key here, but don't mistake this for stubbornness. It's about resiliently holding onto your goals while being flexible about how to reach them. A huge part of the journey is self-reflection, that quiet space where you digest the good, the bad, and the insightful. It's the introspective moment where you recognize what's within your control and accept what's not, only to find a new way forward. Feeling a bit uncomfortable is just a signal that you're stepping into your growth zone, and trust me, that's exactly where you want to be.

Exercises for Building Emotional Strength

Navigating life's ups and downs requires more than just mental acuity; it calls for emotional strength, a kind of resilience that allows us to cope, adapt, and thrive in the face of challenges. You can't always control what happens to you, but you certainly can control how you react. Emotional resilience isn't an inherent trait; it's a skill, and like any skill, it can be developed and refined. In this section, we're going to explore practical, everyday exercises to build your emotional strength. These are your tools; consider them your emotional first-aid kit. They're designed to not only equip you with immediate coping mechanisms but also to instill a lasting mental fortitude. Each exercise is a stepping stone on the path to a more resilient you. Let's get started.

Mindful Observation

Instructions:

- Find a quiet, comfortable space to sit or stand.
- Choose an object within your line of sight.
- Take a deep breath and focus solely on this object for 2–5 minutes.

Mindful observation is a form of meditation that sharpens your ability to concentrate and builds emotional steadiness. By directing your focus toward one object, you train your brain to screen out distractions, making you less susceptible to emotional spirals triggered by outside stressors. It also teaches you to find solace in simplicity, a valuable skill when the world around you seems chaotic. Not to mention, it's a form of grounding that can be used anytime, anywhere. You can even use this technique during stressful work situations by simply focusing on an object on your desk or a feature in the room.

The "AND" Technique

Instructions:

- Identify a strong emotion you're currently feeling.
- Say to yourself, "I'm feeling [emotion] AND..."
- Complete the sentence with another emotion or thought you are also experiencing.

The "AND" Technique is based on the idea that we are capable of feeling more than one emotion simultaneously. It discourages black-and-white thinking, a cognitive distortion that often fuels anxiety and depression. This method encourages you to accept that you can feel anxious AND optimistic or happy AND uncertain. Embracing this emotional duality creates space for nuanced self-reflection, equipping you with a balanced emotional outlook. This practice can be particularly useful in high-stakes situations like job interviews or challenging conversations where emotional clarity can make a significant difference.

Three Good Things

Instructions:

- At the end of each day, take out a notebook or open a digital document.
- Write down three positive things that happened during the day.
- Reflect on each one, even elaborating on why it was important to you.

The power of gratitude can't be overstated. By focusing on what went well, you foster a positive mind frame, which can be a buffer against stress and negativity. Not only does this make you more resilient in the face of adversity, but it also makes your joys more sustainable. Over time, this habit can change your brain's default setting from one of apprehension to one of appreciation, which has long-term benefits for your mental health. Moreover, this practice has the potential to positively influence your relationships, as you'll find yourself acknowledging and appreciating the good in others as well.

The Self-Compassion Letter

Instructions:

- Sit in a quiet space with a pen and paper or a digital writing tool.
- Write a letter to yourself addressing a current challenge or difficulty you're facing.
- Write as if you were talking to a dear friend who is going through the same issue.

It's easy to be hard on ourselves, particularly when facing challenges. Self-compassion is the often-overlooked counterpart to self-esteem. While self-esteem asks, "How can I be better?" self-compassion asks, "How can I be kinder to myself in this moment?" Writing a self-compassion letter allows you to step out of your situation and view it from an external perspective, offering you insights you might have overlooked. This exercise can be an emotional lifeline, giving you the support and courage to take constructive action.

Creative Expression

Instructions:

- Choose a medium you enjoy—drawing, writing, cooking, playing music, and so on.
- Dedicate some uninterrupted time to engage in this creative activity.
- Allow your emotions to flow into what you're creating.

Sometimes, words alone can't capture the full spectrum of our emotions. Engaging in a creative endeavor can act as a cathartic release for emotions that are too complex to articulate. It's a form of self-therapy, allowing you to interpret your feelings without judgment or the need to make sense of them immediately. Over time, you'll find that this exercise not only releases pent-up emotions but also brings you a sense of peace and achievement.

These exercises serve as your emotional gym, and like any form of exercise, the benefits compound over time. What starts as a daily effort will eventually become second nature, transforming not just how you handle adversity, but also how you live your everyday life. It's all about daily commitment, a willingness to confront your emotional blind spots, and the courage to improve and grow stronger.

Wrapping Up

We began this journey with a poignant reminder from Joseph Fort Newton (n.d.): "We cannot tell what may happen to us in the strange medley of life. But we can decide what happens in us—how we can take it, what we do with it—and that is what really counts in the end." You've taken substantial steps toward making what counts, well, truly count.

In this chapter, you've learned

- what emotional resilience is and why it's essential.
- strategies for coping with stress and adversity.
- the importance of a growth mindset in fostering emotional resilience.
- tangible exercises to build emotional strength.

Each of these aspects works in concert to form a well-rounded, emotionally resilient individual. You're learning to be the master of your emotional domain, someone who can not only withstand life's challenges but flourish in spite of them.

But mastering emotional resilience is just one piece of a larger puzzle. It sets the stage for deeper emotional intelligence, a skill set that's essential for living a fulfilling life. Intrigued? Good, because our next chapter dives into Step #4: Cultivating Emotional Intelligence. It's one you won't want to miss as we continue to build upon the sturdy foundation you've already laid.

Case Study: Emma

Emma, a single mother of two, found her world turned upside down with a turbulent divorce and job loss in the wake of an economic downturn. Feeling the weight of these challenges, she found solace in the words of Joseph Fort Newton: "We cannot tell what may happen to us in the strange medley of life. But we can decide what happens in us—how we can take it, what we do with it—and that is what really counts in the end." These words became her guide as she made the conscious decision not just to weather her storms, but to emerge stronger.

In the darkest moments, Emma discovered that emotional resilience was not merely a trait but a dynamic process. She realized it was her ability to adapt and bounce back that empowered her to face life's adversities. She saw herself as a willow tree, bending under strong winds but not breaking. This understanding of emotional resilience came to light not through avoidance but by confronting life's challenges head-on. She leveraged this understanding to cultivate improved coping mechanisms, fortify her relationships, and build a deeper trust in her ability to navigate future life challenges.

Emma realized that emotional strength was not just about enduring hardship but about intelligently navigating through it. She began to see coping skills as her emotional GPS, directing her through the complex terrain of stress and challenges. By identifying her stress triggers and adopting mindfulness practices, she gained control over her emotional responses. She also realized the importance of physical well-being to emotional health and engaged in regular exercise, complemented by professional guidance to manage her emotional landscape more effectively.

As Emma honed her emotional intelligence, she observed a shift in her mindset. She found a strong connection between emotional intelligence and a growth mindset. No longer did she view her setbacks as limitations; they became learning opportunities. The intersection of emotional intelligence and a growth mindset led Emma to a more adaptable and eager approach to life's challenges. She found that her resilience expanded, allowing her to bounce back from setbacks more easily. Through constant reflection, she gradually changed her outlook, embracing life's challenges as opportunities for growth.

To further enhance her emotional resilience, Emma embraced daily practices that seemed simple but were profoundly impactful. For instance, she would engage in a "Why Ladder," a form of self-dialogue where she would repeatedly ask herself 'why' to reach the root cause of her emotional state. She also practiced emotional role-playing, a method where she would mentally rehearse how to respond to different emotional triggers. Another significant practice was maintaining a gratitude journal, which dramatically improved her perspective by focusing on positive aspects of her life.

Case Study: Ericka

Ericka was a powerhouse in the realm of corporate finance, her reputation preceding her in boardrooms across the city. However, when a difficult breakup coincided with unprecedented challenges at work, the walls she had so skillfully built started to crack. Ericka felt lost, with a constant feeling of overwhelm gnawing at her. During a layover at an airport, she picked up a book similar to this one on emotional resilience, almost as if guided by intuition.

As she turned the pages, Ericka felt an immediate connection to the concept. Emotional resilience wasn't about suppressing emotions or slapping on a smile to face the world. It was about the capacity to rebound from setbacks and to adapt in the face of adversity. What struck Ericka was the realization that resilience was the secret sauce to maintaining not only her professional acumen but also her emotional well-being in personal relationships.

Keen to explore this further, she dove into research on effective coping strategies. Gone were the days of drowning her sorrows in wine or losing herself in back-to-back episodes of TV series. Ericka took up mindfulness and meditation. The simple act of focusing on her breath and centering her thoughts allowed her a newfound clarity. She learned to confront, rather than avoid, her stressors, taking them apart piece by piece to better understand and manage them. It wasn't a quick fix, but rather a journey to building an inner arsenal to weather life's ups and downs.

While on this voyage of self-discovery, Ericka also stumbled upon the concept of a growth mindset. It was as if someone had finally put into words what she had long felt but couldn't articulate. The idea of viewing challenges as stepping stones rather than stumbling blocks was transformative. Instead of being shackled by the fear of failure, she embraced it as a learning opportunity, finding value even in the setbacks. Ericka saw how this shift was essential not only for her professional life but for personal growth and emotional well-being, too.

As months turned into a year, the results were nothing short of remarkable. The same job that had once been a constant source of stress became a playground for her newfound resilience and growth mindset. She tackled projects with a nuanced perspective, allowing her to navigate complex negotiations with ease. On the personal front, the emotional void left by her breakup began filling with self-love and a greater appreciation for solitude. Ericka even took to journaling as a form of self-expression and reflection, further solidifying her emotionally resilient foundation.

The most impressive part of her transformation, though, was the undeniable domino effect it had on all aspects of her life. Relationships were healthier; her professional life flourished even more, and above all, Ericka found a deep-rooted sense of contentment and joy. The constant anxiety that used to cloud her thoughts like a lingering fog had lifted, replaced by the sunny skies of emotional freedom.

Ericka's journey wasn't just a series of fortunate events or a lucky break; it was a calculated, conscious effort to develop a skill set that ultimately reshaped her world. So, if you're standing at the edge, wondering how to traverse the choppy waters of life, channel Ericka and live your best life.

FOUR

Step #4—Enhancing Your Social Skills

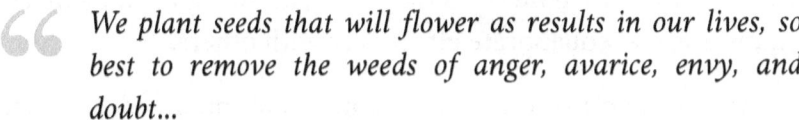 *We plant seeds that will flower as results in our lives, so best to remove the weeds of anger, avarice, envy, and doubt...*

Dorothy Day

The wisdom of Dorothy Day serves as a gentle reminder that our actions and interactions carry long-lasting repercussions, shaping the quality of our lives and those around us. Just as a gardener carefully tends to each bud, leaf, and stem, we, too, must cultivate our social skills to yield a harvest rich in meaningful connections, self-understanding, and collective well-being.

Welcome to Step #4: Enhancing Your Social Skills. Here, we'll confront some of the most common obstacles you may face in interpersonal situations and provide practical tips for turning awkward moments into opportunities for genuine connection. Our goal? To equip you with the skills necessary for optimized levels of emotional intelligence. By nurturing these skills, you not only improve your life but also sow seeds of kindness, empathy, and understanding in the world around you.

So, if you've ever found yourself tongue-tied at parties, misunderstood in meetings, or simply longing for deeper, more enriching relationships, this chapter is for you. Let's start sowing those seeds and watch how they transform your emotional landscape.

The Relationship Between Social Skills and Emotional Intelligence

The relationship between social skills and emotional intelligence is deeply intertwined, much like the roots and branches of a sturdy tree. If emotional intelligence is the root system—giving us stability, nourishment, and a strong foundation—then social skills are the branches that reach out into the world, allowing us to connect, communicate, and collaborate effectively with others.

In Daniel Goleman's framework of emotional intelligence, social skills are considered one of the five critical components (Goleman, 2021). They are the outward manifestation of our internal emotional competencies. While other elements like self-awareness, self-regulation, and empathy help us understand and manage our own emotions, social skills translate that internal understanding into external action. They enable us to navigate complex social situations and foster positive relationships, both of which are critical in reaching our personal and professional goals.

Social skills aren't just about making small talk or mastering the art of conversation. They encompass a wide array of competencies like active listening, conflict resolution, and even leadership abilities. These skills, when honed, contribute to higher emotional intelligence as they require a deep understanding of both self and others. In other words, effective social skills require you to tap into your emotional intelligence to perceive, evaluate, and respond to social cues in a way that is both genuine and constructive.

Emotional intelligence and social skills are two sides of the same coin. One is inward-facing, helping us to understand ourselves, while the other is outward-facing, enabling us to engage with the world around us. Together, they create a harmonious cycle where improved emotional intelligence leads to better social skills, and better social skills, in turn, enhance our emotional intelligence. So, as we work on developing one, we invariably enrich the other, creating a life that's both emotionally rewarding and socially fulfilling.

The Importance of Effective Communication

Communication is not just a skill; it's an art form. It's not merely a transaction where one person talks and the other listens. It's an interaction, a dialogue where both parties are fully present. So, let's talk about what we mean by effective communication. It's not about using ten-dollar words or mastering the art of persuasion. It's about connecting authentically and being yourself while allowing others the same privilege.

True communication has depth; it's about leaning into the discomfort to say what you mean, but also pausing to really hear what someone else is trying to say. We've all experienced those precious moments when we feel genuinely seen and heard—those are the exchanges that stay with us, the ones that forge bonds and deepen our understanding of not only others but ourselves.

Let's shift the way we think about this. It's not just about "telling and receiving," but rather, it's about "sharing and co-creating." Don't just share your point of view; share yourself. And don't just take in information; become a part of the narrative, share your story, and connect. This doesn't happen overnight; it takes practice and a willingness to mess up and try again. But when we invest in truly understanding this art form, we enrich our own lives and the lives of those around us.

Benefits of Effective Communication

The quality of our relationships, whether at work or home, is often mirrored by the quality of our communication. When you can talk openly, when you can show up authentically and let others do the same, you lay down the bricks for a bridge that's both strong and flexible. This isn't just about knowing when to speak; it's also about knowing when to listen, when to ask questions, and when to simply be there, offering your presence as the most profound form of support. This mutual exchange, this give-and-take, is like a duet that nurtures not just a relationship but individual growth.

Helps Handle Conflicts Better

Conflict. The word alone might make your heart rate jump a little. But what if we saw conflict not as a crisis but as an opportunity? An opportunity to deepen our understanding, to fine-tune our empathy, to refine the edges of our own self-awareness? Effective communication lets us do that. It's the framework that allows us to navigate disagreements with integrity and to hash things out without tearing each other down. It's about leaning into the discomfort, not with armor, but with openness. And when we approach conflict this way, we come out the other side stronger and wiser.

Builds Empathy

If there's one thing we're starved for in this world, it's empathy. We don't just need to recognize it; we need to cultivate it like our lives depend on it—because they do. Empathy is the emotional currency that enriches our inner lives and sweetens our social interactions. Effective communication lets us do more than put ourselves in someone else's shoes—it lets us walk in them. When you truly listen to understand, not just to respond, you're not just hearing words; you're touching a soul. This kind of soul-to-soul connection creates a shared space for true compassion to bloom.

Increases Self-Awareness

The journey toward effective communication is not just outward; it's also inward. As we get better at engaging with others, we simultaneously unveil layers of our own inner world. Self-awareness isn't merely a byproduct of good communication; it's a cornerstone. How can you share yourself authentically if you haven't first confronted your own complexities? The more we know ourselves, the better we communicate, and vice versa.

Builds Trust

Trust is more than just a five-letter word; it's the invisible glue that holds our social fabric together. Trust isn't a commodity you can buy or a favor you can trade. It's earned, and the currency we use is genuine, transparent communication. When you can speak your truth and allow others to speak theirs, when you can disagree without being disagreeable, when you can be vulnerable without feeling weak—that's when trust blossoms. It becomes the solid foundation on which all other virtues can stand.

So, there it is—effective communication is not just a skill to be acquired. It's a path to a richer, more resonant life.

Active Listening Techniques

Listening isn't just about hearing words. We're all pretty good at nodding while mentally composing our grocery list. But here's the deal—active listening is about creating a spacious room in your mind and inviting someone else's words to come and dance. It's a whole different league from what we call "passive listening," which is that nod-and-smile routine we're all too familiar with.

In passive listening, your ears might catch the sound, but your heart misses the emotion, and your brain misses the nuance. Active listening is an intentional act. You make a deliberate choice to give your undivided attention, to dive into the conversation not as a spectator, but as an engaged participant. It's about making eye contact, providing feedback, and asking probing questions that dig deeper into the discussion. You're not just on the receiving end of communication; you're an active collaborator in the process.

So, why does this matter? Well, active listening isn't just a technique; it's a way of being in the world. It's how you invite more depth into your interactions and how you cultivate that elusive treasure we call "understanding." Whether you're negotiating a contract, deepening a friendship, or trying to see eye-to-eye with a family member, active listening is your best friend. It equips you with the tools to dig for the treasures often buried in the hills of our daily dialogues. So yes, let's aim to do more than just hear. Let's listen—actively.

How to Listen Actively

When you listen actively, you're not just lending an ear; you're lending your whole self. Your mind isn't elsewhere; it's right there, in the conversation. Think about the people who have really listened to you in your life. How did they make you feel? Heard, valued, respected—right? That's the gift you can offer to someone when you truly engage in active listening.

Face the Speaker and Have Eye Contact

The art of active listening starts with positioning yourself to fully engage with the speaker. When you face the speaker and maintain eye contact, you're not just observing; you're participating in the conversation. This simple but intentional action can powerfully communicate that you're present and interested. In turn, it encourages the speaker to be more open, fostering a dialogue that is more genuine and productive. In essence, your body language sets the stage for meaningful communication.

"Listen" to Non-Verbal Cues Too

While spoken words carry the crux of the message, there's a parallel conversation happening through non-verbal cues. Gestures, facial expressions, and even pauses contribute significantly to the message. Being attentive to these subtleties offers you a more nuanced understanding of the discussion. It's like reading between the lines; you get the full story, not just the summary. Your awareness of these cues also shows the speaker that you genuinely care about what they're saying beyond just the words they use.

Don't Interrupt

Resisting the temptation to interrupt is a cornerstone of active listening. Interruptions can disrupt the flow of the conversation and may prevent the speaker from getting to the core of their message. By keeping silent at the right times, you're handing the speaker a figurative microphone, saying, "This is your stage, your moment. I'm here to listen." It's a simple yet profound way to show respect and open-mindedness.

Listen Without Judging or Jumping to Conclusions

When you listen without preconceived judgments or the impulse to draw early conclusions, you create a space where open and honest communication can take place. Imagine your mind as a blank slate, open to various colors and forms. By keeping your internal commentary at bay, you allow the speaker to freely express their thoughts and feelings. You're essentially saying, "I'm here to understand you, not to judge or solve you."

Don't Start Planning What to Say Next

As tempting as it is to plan your next sentence or rebuttal, doing so takes you out of the moment. The magic of active listening lies in genuine presence. By focusing entirely on what's being said, you increase your understanding of the speaker's point of view. You'll also find that when you listen closely, your appropriate response often naturally emerges from the conversation itself without pre-planning.

Don't Impose Your Opinions or Solutions

Even if you think you've got the perfect advice or solution, hold off on sharing it unless you're asked. Offering unsolicited advice can inadvertently send the message that you're not really listening, but rather waiting for your turn to speak. When you listen without imposing your own opinions, you're showing the speaker that their thoughts and feelings are valid, fostering a more supportive environment.

Stay Focused

A wandering mind is a common obstacle to active listening. If you find your attention drifting, gently bring it back to the conversation at hand. Mindfulness techniques, such as focusing on your breath, can be helpful in keeping you anchored. Your focus is a gift to the speaker and yourself; it enriches the conversation and your relationships.

Ask Questions

Inquiring for clarification or elaboration not only shows your interest but can also uncover deeper layers of the topic at hand. It tells the speaker, "I care enough to understand this fully." It's an extension of active listening and adds another dimension to the conversation. Asking questions helps you both dig deeper, turning a superficial chat into a meaningful dialogue.

Practicing these techniques can transform your conversations from mundane exchanges to enriching experiences, bringing benefits that ripple out into all areas of your life.

Types of Non-Verbal Communication

Let's take a moment to appreciate the unspoken dimensions of our conversations—the way our bodies "speak" even when we're silent. Non-verbal communication is the wordless exchange that happens alongside or instead of verbal dialogue. It's a symphony of facial expressions, gestures, eye contact, posture, and even the distance we keep from each other. But don't mistake its silence for simplicity. Non-verbal cues are complex and multifaceted, often expressing emotions or intentions that words may not fully capture.

It's fascinating how non-verbal communication can differ across cultures, yet some fundamental elements—like a smile—seem to be universally understood. Your eyes, for instance, can reveal excitement or boredom, curiosity or indifference. And let's not forget the eloquence of the hands. From a simple thumbs-up to a complex dance of gestures during an animated chat, our hands often talk as much as our mouths do.

Even the space we occupy says something. The distance you keep from someone can indicate intimacy or formality, comfort, or unease. Sometimes, the silence between your words can be just as telling. A prolonged silence might indicate contemplation, awkwardness, or even a shared understanding that needs no words. And let's not overlook the role of touch—a pat on the back, a hug, or even a high-five can speak volumes.

Each of these non-verbal elements contributes to the message we're conveying. If they're in harmony with our spoken words, they enhance understanding and trust. But if they clash, they can create confusion or suspicion. For example, if you say you're fine but your face looks strained, people might doubt your words and wonder what's really going on.

How to Build It

The beautiful thing about skills is that they can be honed, and non-verbal communication is no exception. It's like working on a canvas, each brushstroke improving the overall picture. Let's go through some practical ways to refine this art of silent conversation.

Make Proper Eye Contact

The eyes aren't just the window to the soul; they're a billboard that advertises your attentiveness and sincerity. Establishing solid eye contact shows that you're engaged and interested. However, it's crucial to find a balance; constant staring can be intimidating, while too little can seem dismissive. Start by observing how people respond to your eye contact and adjust accordingly. Aim for meaningful glances that invite connection without overwhelming the other person.

Be Aware of Body Language

Your body can be a powerful spokesperson, speaking volumes without uttering a word. Posture, for example, can indicate confidence or insecurity, openness or defensiveness. The key is self-awareness. Are your arms crossed in a way that might appear defensive? Is your stance inviting or standoffish? Observe others and then bring that same discerning eye to your own body language.

Facial Expressions Don't Lie

There's a wealth of information on your face, whether it's a smirk, a frown, or a wide-eyed look of surprise. Emotions play across our faces like a slideshow, offering clues about our feelings and thoughts. Take note of your facial expressions during different situations. Are you furrowing your brows when confused? Smiling when pleased? Your face tells a story; make sure it's one you want to share.

Play With Your Tone of Voice

Voice can carry an emotional payload just as heavy as any word or phrase. Volume, pitch, and speed all play a part in how our verbal communications are received. If you've ever found yourself saying, "It's not what you said; it's how you said it," you understand the impact tone can have. Experiment with different vocal nuances to discover how they can alter the meaning of your words and affect your interactions.

Pay Attention to Discrepancies in Behavior

We've all met people whose words say one thing, but their non-verbal cues say another. It creates discord that can be off-putting or confusing. The same can happen in reverse; maybe you're saying you're open to feedback, but your crossed arms and stern face suggest otherwise. It's crucial to align your verbal and non-verbal communications for clarity and authenticity.

When in Doubt, Ask

If you find that you're not sure how your non-verbal cues are landing or you're confused by someone else's, there's no shame in seeking clarification. Open dialogue about your observations can dispel misunderstandings and pave the way for more meaningful connections.

Practice Makes Perfect

Just like learning a musical instrument or a new language, improving your non-verbal communication skills will take time and practice. Experiment in different social settings, be it a family gathering or a business meeting. Keep tweaking and adjusting until you find your rhythm.

In essence, your non-verbal cues can either be the harmony that elevates the song of your interactions or the dissonance that confuses your message. Taking the time to improve these skills can lead to richer, more authentic connections with others.

Building Rapport and Positive Relationships

In the realm of emotional intelligence and social skills, rapport goes beyond mere friendship—it's an alignment of emotional energies, a certain synergy of soul. When you're in rapport with someone, there's a mutual understanding, a shared wavelength. You're not just talking; you're connecting.

Building rapport isn't a mere transaction; it's more like growing a garden. You can't force a plant to grow, but you can provide it with the soil, water, and sunlight it needs to flourish. Similarly, rapport blossoms in an environment of mutual respect, shared values, and open communication.

How does one go about nurturing this harmonious relationship? Well, the art of building rapport is part of the "R" in RAIN Selling methodology, which stands for building rapport, asking questions, identifying needs, and establishing the next steps (Schultz, 2019). In essence, if you want to build rapport, it starts with making a genuine human connection, understanding the other person's needs, and valuing the relationship more than the transaction at hand.

So, the next time you find yourself in a social setting, be it a dinner party, a networking event, or just a simple conversation with a stranger, remember that rapport is your golden key to unlocking deeper connections. With a little effort and emotional intelligence, you can turn surface-level interactions into relationships that are rich, rewarding, and mutually beneficial.

How to Build Rapport

So, you've decided to make rapport-building a priority—that's a big win in the realm of social skills. The first step toward building strong relationships is wanting to create them and being intentional about it. Let's dig into the specifics now.

Make a Good Introduction

Before you can begin to build rapport, you've got to break the ice. Your introduction serves as your first impression. So, make it count. It doesn't have to be elaborate; a warm smile, a firm (but not crushing) handshake, and a simple "Hi, I'm [Your Name], nice to meet you" can go a long way.

Actively Listen

Remember, rapport isn't just about talking; it's about listening—really listening. This means not just hearing the words but understanding the emotions and intentions behind them. Active listening is a conscious effort that involves empathy, patience, and sometimes, even biting your tongue. When you show that you're invested in understanding the other person's point of view, you pave the way for a more meaningful connection.

Ask Engaging Questions

Once you've opened the door, keep the conversation going by asking questions that provoke thought and elicit more than a simple "yes" or "no" answer. Open-ended questions like "What brings you here?" or "How do you feel about [topic]?" can offer more room for dialogue and help you learn more about the other person's thoughts and feelings.

Be Aware of Your Body Language

We communicate not just through words, but also through our bodies. So, stand tall, make eye contact, and offer open and inviting gestures. Your non-verbal cues can either reinforce what you're saying or contradict it, so aligning both is crucial to build rapport.

Find Commonalities

Finding common ground can serve as a quick shortcut to rapport. Whether it's a shared interest, a mutual friend, or even a common struggle, these shared experiences can create an instant bond. It's like finding out you both love the same obscure band; it instantly takes the relationship to the next level.

Lead With Empathy and Respect

This is the cornerstone of any strong relationship. If you can put yourself in the other person's shoes and show them respect regardless of the situation, you're well on your way to building rapport that will last.

Building rapport isn't just a one-time effort; it's a continuing process that benefits not just you, but everyone around you. It turns ordinary interactions into memorable ones and acquaintances into genuine friendships. So go ahead, take the plunge, and make building rapport your second nature. You won't regret it.

Wrapping Up

Just as Dorothy Day reminds us, "We plant seeds that will flower as results in our lives, so best to remove the weeds of anger, avarice, envy and doubt..." Well, my friends, we've been busy gardeners in this chapter, sowing seeds of better social interactions and nurturing the ground for deeper connections.

What we've covered:

- Importance of social skills: We discovered that social skills are not just a "nice-to-have" but essential for better emotional intelligence.
- Effective communication: From verbal exchanges to non-verbal cues, we peeled back the layers of what it really means to communicate well.
- Active listening: We went beyond the usual "nod and smile" to truly understand and empathize with others.
- Building rapport: A deeper dive into forming meaningful relationships by being respectful, showing empathy, and finding common ground.

With each conversation, each meaningful glance, and each genuine interaction, we're cultivating a garden teeming with the flowers of better emotional health, resilience, and yes, even happiness. But let's not get too comfortable just yet; the world of emotional intelligence is vast and filled with possibilities.

In the next chapter, we're going to explore another crucial aspect of emotional intelligence: self-awareness. This is the root system of our garden, nourishing and supporting everything else we've planted.

Case Study: Alan

Imagine sitting down for coffee with Alan, an IT manager who's aced every technical skill but still feels like something's missing. Alan's got a hunch that his social skills, or lack thereof, are the missing link. So, he decides it's time for a change. This isn't just a story of how Alan climbed the corporate ladder; it's a story of how he became a better listener, a more compassionate friend, and a more intuitive leader.

Alan started where we all should: he got curious about the role of emotional intelligence in social skills. You see, social skills aren't about how many jokes you can tell at a party. They're grounded in emotional intelligence—our ability to read, understand, and respond to emotions in ourselves and others. Alan soon understood that to connect better with people, he had to connect better with himself. It's that soul-deep stuff we often want to dodge but can't afford to.

Now, about communication. Alan thought he was a good communicator, but he came to see that effective communication is a two-way street. You send out a message, and you receive one back; in between is a whole universe of perception, emotion, and interpretation. Alan practiced active listening, a kind of listening where you're not just hearing words but understanding the feelings and intentions behind them.

Alan also discovered the silent but vital role of non-verbal communication. We're talking about the unspoken conversation our bodies are having while our mouths are moving. Our eyes, our facial expressions, and even our posture spill secrets about our true thoughts and feelings. Alan put effort into this quiet dialogue, making sure his body wasn't sending out messages he didn't intend.

Then came the magic of building rapport. Alan was put in charge of a project and decided to apply what he'd learned. He didn't walk into the room as just a manager but as a person genuinely interested in the well-being of his team. He led with empathy, created a space for open communication, and found common ground. His project didn't just meet targets; it soared. And so did Alan. He got a well-deserved promotion and, more importantly, a deeper, more fulfilling connection with those around him.

What Alan learned, and what we've explored here, is that emotional intelligence isn't just a nice-to-have; it's a game-changer. Alan became the hero of his own story, and you can too.

Case Study: Jane

Jane was a pro at her job, navigating spreadsheets and meetings like a champion. Yet, despite her career success, her personal relationships felt superficial. The absence of a deeper emotional connection with her friends, family, and even colleagues was something she couldn't shake off. Then she stumbled upon the idea of emotional intelligence—this intriguing blend of self-awareness and social skills that seemed to be the missing link in her life.

The notion that emotional intelligence is the bedrock upon which social skills are built intrigued her. She started seeing social dynamics in a whole new light. This wasn't about having a vast network of contacts; it was about truly connecting with people, understanding their emotions, and, even more importantly, understanding her own. Emotional intelligence taught her to tune into the emotional nuances in conversations and to navigate interpersonal relationships more sensitively.

But she also learned that effective communication is more than a two-way street—it's a highway built on mutual understanding and respect. She came to see it as an art form. For her, it wasn't just about saying the right things but also ensuring that the other person genuinely understood her and felt understood themselves. This shift in perspective took her interactions from transactional to transformational.

Once she adopted this more nuanced approach to communication, a magical thing happened: her relationships began to flourish. Not just in the 'let's get coffee sometime' sort of way, but genuinely meaningful connections formed. She found it easier to resolve conflicts, not just by finding a solution but by understanding the emotional core of the issue. Empathy wasn't just a word; it was a practice, helping her to step into other people's shoes to feel what they felt. The awareness she developed about her own communication style made her more adaptable, instilling a greater sense of trust among those she interacted with.

Then, there was the discovery of active listening. For Jane, listening had always been a passive activity—something she did in between her turns to speak. She learned the power of truly hearing someone, not just waiting for her chance to reply. This meant maintaining eye contact, reading non-verbal cues like the tilt of a head or the fold of arms, and resisting the urge to interrupt or impose her own solutions. The quality of her conversations skyrocketed, as did the satisfaction she and others got from them.

Of course, the role of non-verbal communication became evident, too. She realized she'd been ignoring a whole channel of human interaction by not focusing on things like eye contact, body language, and even the tone of her voice. A furrowed brow or a dissonant tone could undo even the most well-chosen words. She practiced aligning her body language with her feelings, making her not only more authentic but also easier to understand.

Lastly, she dabbled in the art of rapport. She found that it's one thing to have a conversation and another to have a meaningful connection. Rapport was the secret sauce that turned ordinary interactions into memorable ones. She became a pro at not just talking, but engaging—making a fantastic first impression, keeping conversations alive with great questions, and establishing common ground with just about anyone.

All these little changes started adding up. Jane became the person people could confide in, seek advice from, and genuinely enjoy spending time with. She moved beyond being just competent at her job; she became a true leader—someone who led with emotional wisdom rather than just expertise. But most of all, she found that her relationships, which had always felt like a missing puzzle piece in her life, were now her greatest joy and strength. It was as if she had discovered a hidden layer of life, one that had always been there but she had never seen. And all it took was the willingness to venture beyond her comfort zone and invest in the soft skills that ended up making the biggest difference in her life.

Sharing the Power of Emotional Intelligence

"We cannot tell what may happen to us in the strange medley of life. But we can decide what happens in us — how we can take it, what we do with it — and that is what really counts in the end."

Joseph Fort Newton

Emotional hurricanes affect us all at some point in our lives, and until we know how to take charge and hone our emotional intelligence, they can be very difficult to climb out of.

Relationships end... Things happen at work... Disagreements find their way into families and friendship groups... We're ambushed by money worries... Life will always throw challenges our way, and with most of them comes a healthy dose of emotional turbulence.

We'll never be able to stop that from happening, but we can change our reactions, improving our connection with and understanding of others at the same time. As you'll see once you start putting all of this into practice, it's a game-changer, and it becomes much easier to soak up all the joy life has to offer instead of getting bogged down by all the challenges.

Emotional intelligence is a powerful tool, and it can have such a profound impact on your life that I want to help as many people as I can to develop theirs. And this is where I'd like to ask for your help. Don't worry – it won't take long. All I'd like you to do is take a few minutes to spread the word.

By leaving a review of this book on Amazon, you'll direct other people who crave this guidance straight to what they're looking for.

Every review acts as a lighthouse, guiding those who are already searching for the information towards the help they need.

Thank you so much for your support. Life will never stop throwing challenges at us, so it's up to us to take charge.

Scan the QR code below

FIVE

Step #5—Cultivating Empathy

 Emotions are enmeshed in the neural networks of reason.

Antonio Dumasio

That quote from neuroscientist Antonio Damasio really resonates—our emotions and reasoning abilities are tied together. How we feel affects how we think. This connection is at the core of what it means to cultivate empathy.

Empathy is about seeing things from another person's perspective, stepping into their shoes, looking through their eyes, and trying to understand their experiences and feelings. Easier said than done, right? We all have our own biases and worldviews that make it challenging to connect on that deeper level.

In this chapter, we'll talk about the common roadblocks to empathy—the tendency to judge quickly, the failure to listen closely, and the lack of curiosity about different viewpoints. However, empathy is a skill we can develop with practice and intention. The rewards make the effort worthwhile.

Imagine how empathy could transform your relationships and daily interactions. Understanding someone's emotions allows you to relate to them in a more genuine way. You build trust and compassion. Conflicts can be resolved by seeking common ground. Even our relationships with ourselves can benefit from self-empathy—understanding rather than criticizing our own feelings and experiences.

I'll share proven techniques to help build your "empathy muscles," making perspective-taking more natural over time. Small mindset shifts that encourage you to listen fully, suspend judgment, and find shared human experiences with those around you. Together, we'll explore this powerful tool for fostering kinder, more caring connections.

What Is Empathy?

What is empathy, you ask? It's about connecting to that voice inside all of us that says, "You are seen; you matter." Empathy means opening your spirit to let someone else's light shine in. It's the practice of slipping into their shoes, seeing through their eyes, and walking with them heart-to-heart. When you make space for empathy, you make space for growth, wisdom, and understanding.

Empathy illuminates. When you make the effort to view the world from another's perspective, walls crumble. Conflicts dissolve into mutual understanding. Empathy breeds compassion. It whispers—we are more alike than different, you and I. With empathy as your guide, you move through the world with more patience, more kindness, and more care.

Cultivating empathy elevates your emotional intelligence. Emotional intelligence is the language of the heart—understanding what the heart needs and then speaking its truth with courage and kindness. Empathy fluency is vital. The more empathy flows freely, the wiser our words and actions become. Empathy connects you to your highest self.

At its core, empathy is recognizing the humanity in each of us. It's saying I see you; I feel you; I care. Practicing empathy connects us at a soul level. It lights the path to hope, healing, and a more conscious way of living. When you lead with empathy, you lead with love.

So, nurture your empathy. Let it be a north star guiding you toward deeper self-discovery, richer relationships, and a world united through the power of compassion. When we lead with the heart, we lift humanity. Empathy begets empathy. Spread it generously and watch it multiply.

Steps to Become More Empathetic

The journey to greater empathy starts with curiosity. Make an effort to open your heart to those around you, even strangers or people you perceive as different. Seek to understand their unique stories. When we awaken to each other's inner light with openness, empathy begins to flow more freely.

Focus your awareness on the similarities between yourself and others rather than the differences. Underneath it all, we are more alike than different—we all hope, hurt, and dream. We all desire purpose, belonging, and love. Our shared human experiences far outweigh surface distinctions.

Practice slipping into the shoes of others often. Imagine how their decisions, words, and actions impact those around them from their perspective. When you make the effort to know someone's pain, you become better equipped to offer comfort or support. Walk the path with them in spirit.

Listen deeply and attentively when interacting with others. Offer them your true, uninterrupted presence. Then, share your own experiences vulnerable, too. The door to connection and understanding swings both ways.

Consider joining hands with those marching for justice, equality, and inclusion—causes aimed at lifting up the voices left unheard. In struggle, we evolve. Through service, we transform. Uplifting others uplifts our shared humanity.

Get creative in your quest for empathy. Write stories, draw, play roles, or explore new perspectives through any form of artistry. The heart reveals itself to an open, curious mind. There are infinite paths to walk in another's shoes.

Empathy's river runs deep. Wade into it. Make small efforts to nurture empathy each day. Let it flow freely through you, washing away judgment and misunderstandings. With radical openness, empathy ignites revolution.

Overcoming Barriers to Empathy

Our fast-paced, disconnected world builds barriers to empathy—but we can dismantle them with patience and intention. Judging too quickly and listening poorly. Fearing differences, these patterns block empathy's flow. When we fail to see each other's humanity, we all suffer.

Slow down, breathe deep. Make time for real connection. Reserve judgment—we all have reasons for our beliefs. Listen fully to understand, not just respond. Seek the shared inner experiences behind surface differences. At our core, we are more alike than different—all deserving of compassion.

Practice gratitude, even for those who challenge you. Thank them for new perspectives. Discomfort opens the mind if you embrace it. Lead with compassion always, even when met with anger. Fighting fire with fire only burns everyone in the end. Stay steady, sharing empathy.

Reflect often on times you felt unheard or misunderstood. Let those memories open your heart to others struggling now. Hurt people inevitably hurt more people. But healed people can choose to heal. Shine light where you found darkness.

Meditate frequently on our interdependence. We need each other now more than ever before. We rise or fall as one people. Empathy is the thread weaving us together into a tapestry of hope. Stay vigilant in mending rips and holes with care.

So, silence the inner critic. Adopt a beginner's mind in every encounter. Make space for empathy to enter. Let it soften hardened edges over time. Stay endlessly curious and endlessly humble. We all have more to learn than we could ever teach.

With empathy's grace, we build bridges. We cease to "other"-ize those unlike us. Inequities are righted, divisions healed. Open hands give and open hearts receive. When I walk in your shoes, you walk in mine. We carry each other's burdens, sharing the load.

Real-World Scenarios for Practicing Empathy

Bridging life's inevitable chasms between us requires opening our hearts to empathy. In the workplace, as in life, opportunities abound to exercise this core human capacity. When we meet each other with radical compassion, even brief interactions can affirm our shared humanity.

The following cases illustrate the power of empathy to heal and connect, even in everyday workplace scenarios. You will read about managers who listened empathetically to struggling team members rather than criticizing from a distance; coworkers who grieved together after a painful loss; and people who found common ground after conflict through vulnerability.

Each example provides a blueprint for weaving more empathy into your daily professional relationships. By suspending judgment, finding commonality, and simply listening with care to colleagues, you, too, can build trust, resolve tensions, and lift others up. With consistent practice, empathy becomes second nature.

The deepest business insights are human insights. These stories reveal that we are not robots checking tasks off a list. We are complex beings seeking purpose and compassion right alongside profitability. When you look past job titles to see the whole human, empathy transforms how you lead, collaborate, and support each other through life's ups and downs.

Sanjay and Alicia

It had been a long, stressful week and tempers were running high on the team. As project manager, I noticed tension brewing between two of my team members, Sanjay and Alicia. They had clashed over project priorities in our last meeting.

I scheduled time to speak privately with each person. With Alicia, I asked how she was feeling about the team dynamic. She confided that she felt dismissed and unheard by Sanjay in meetings. I reflected her feelings back to ensure she felt understood. We discussed her preferred working style and needs.

Next, I met with Sanjay. Rather than criticizing him, I focused on understanding his perspective. He shared feeling overwhelmed and micromanaged lately. I expressed empathy for his situation and asked collaborative questions about what support he needed.

In our 1-on-1s, I simply listened empathetically, resisting the urge to problem-solve immediately. Providing them each a non-judgmental space to share their experiences was powerful. They both felt heard and validated.

At our next team meeting, the mood was far lighter. By leading with empathy, I helped dissolve tension. We determined project priorities together, valuing all voices and ideas equally. My empathy helped their empathy bloom in turn.

Kate

When our team suddenly shifted to remote work during the pandemic, I noticed Kate struggling in our online meetings. She was once lively and outgoing, now quiet and withdrawn. I sensed something deeper was amiss.

Rather than criticizing her disengagement, I decided to have an empathetic conversation. Kate revealed she was feeling extremely isolated, guilty about managing her kids' virtual schooling, and burnt out.

I related to those emotions, sharing my own challenges as a working parent right now. We discussed ways to modify her workload and increase flexibility. I asked how I could better support her needs on our distributed team. Kate felt genuinely heard and cared for.

In our 1-on-1s going forward, I made an effort to check in on Kate's well-being, not just project status. We built-in social time before meetings. I publicly thanked her for her contributions, big and small.

Kate's demeanor improved dramatically. She regained her characteristic zeal and humor. By extending empathy about a difficult situation, I helped Kate feel valued, empowered, and optimistic.

James

When my friend James lost his mom, I could feel the weight of his grief from across the room. I knew that words like "I'm sorry for your loss" wouldn't be enough. Not for this. I also sensed that James needed room to breathe, but how could I reach out without making him feel cornered?

We decided to go for a walk; fresh air has a way of loosening the emotional knots in our chests. So, there we were, the sky stretching out above us as we ventured into the deeper realms of our friendship. I chose to ask him questions about his mom that invited stories rather than yes-or-no answers. What was your favorite thing about her? Do you remember any advice she gave you that sticks out? James's face lit up, and the stories flowed. His eyes sparkled as he shared memories that I could tell were windows into the love he had for her.

He let it slip that in other conversations he'd had, he felt obligated to shelve his grief like some uninvited guest. Hearing this broke my heart. No one should have to closet their grief, especially not for something as inconsequential as workplace etiquette. I told him we could manage without him having to put on a brave face all the time. "We get it, man. Take the time you need. And hey, if it helps, I can take some stuff off your plate for the next little while."

By giving him that space to be unapologetically himself, to feel what he was going through without having to explain or justify it, I hoped to offer a kind of sanctuary. We talked about how to make his life a little easier while he navigated through his grief. Simple things, like helping with meals and taking walks, so he didn't feel alone.

James thanked me for our walk-and-talk with a sincerity that hit me deep. "You have no idea how much this conversation means to me," he said. In that moment, I realized that empathy isn't just a nice-to-have quality; it's a must-have. We all carry our private struggles, our hidden stories that make us who we are. When we choose empathy, we choose to honor those stories in each other. We go from being people who merely coexist to people who deeply understand and, in that understanding, find a connection that is as humbling as it is profound.

Wrapping up

"Emotions are enmeshed in the neural networks of reason." As neuroscientist Antonio Damasio astutely noted, empathy lives at the intersection of heart and mind.

In this chapter, we explored the incredible value of cultivating empathy and practical steps to grow this capacity, including:

- listening deeply without judgment
- taking time to understand different perspectives
- finding common ground and shared experiences
- overcoming biases and barriers through self-reflection
- leading with compassion even when met with anger

By integrating empathy into your daily thoughts and actions, you positively transform relationships and nurture community. Start small—next time, instead of instant analysis, offer someone your ear. When you stand in their shoes, you just may find you're on the same journey after all.

Now that we've opened our minds to empathy, we'll turn in the next chapter to deepening self-awareness. Knowing ourselves allows us to show up fully for others. Onward in our quest for emotional wisdom!

Case Study: Emily

Picture this: Emily, a high-flying executive known for her razor-sharp analysis and focus on results. She was top of her game but still felt like something was missing. During a routine check-in, her mentor suggested that what could elevate her leadership even further was cultivating empathy. Emily was initially puzzled. Empathy? Wasn't that just a touchy-feely thing? She decided to dig deeper, realizing that empathy was more than just a warm, fuzzy idea. It was a vital leadership quality that could reshape not only her career but also her life.

The thing about empathy was that it was a complex dance of emotional and cognitive understanding. It was the kind of skill that wove into every aspect of our lives, from our relationships to our work. In a world often drowning in conflict and disconnection, empathy was the lifeboat. Emily began to see that empathy was like the soulmate of emotional intelligence. It wasn't just about understanding your own emotions, but truly feeling and grasping the emotional landscape of others.

With her new knowledge, Emily decided to shake things up at work. She became curious about her colleagues beyond the scope of their professional roles. In meetings, she noticed their body language, heard the hesitations in their voice, and asked questions that invited real, honest answers. Emily realized that focusing on similarities rather than differences brought a team together like nothing else.

She then dove deeper, determined to conquer her own barriers to empathy. She once believed that to be empathetic meant you had to be an open book, which for her felt risky. She learned that empathy wasn't about oversharing but finding a balanced way to listen and be heard, to understand and be understood. It wasn't all rose-tinted; Emily acknowledged that biases and judgments could get in her way. She started practicing mindfulness to help her notice when these barriers were showing up and challenged herself to overcome them.

In a matter of months, Emily witnessed a transformation. Her team was more cohesive, and their productivity had skyrocketed. But more importantly, her relationships—both professional and personal—were richer and more meaningful. Emily became an advocate for social causes she'd previously overlooked, recognizing that empathy didn't stop at the office door; it was a way of being in the world.

So here is the heart of it: When you cultivate empathy, you aren't just becoming a better colleague or a better leader; you become a better human. The landscape of your life transforms, and suddenly, your path seems clearer and more purposeful. It is as if the universe was inviting you to a bigger, richer narrative. That is a pretty powerful outcome.

Case Study: Remigio

Remigio, a high school teacher with a no-nonsense reputation, found himself at a crossroads. He was respected, yes, but he was also distant from his students. Despite the high test scores and the disciplined classroom environment, something essential was missing. He sensed that he was failing to connect with his students on a human level. This emotional disconnect was not just in his professional life; it trickled into his personal relationships, too.

Fueled by the unease he felt, Remigio started reading up on emotional intelligence and empathy. At first, he was a bit skeptical. Could these "soft skills" really make a significant difference? Would diving into emotions not make his classroom a mess?

Challenging his own reservations, he started a small experiment. He made it a point to genuinely ask students about their lives, their aspirations, and their worries. No longer was his classroom solely a platform for lectures; it became a stage for shared human experiences.

The transformation didn't happen overnight. Old habits die hard, as they say, and Remigio found himself occasionally slipping back into his old pattern of detached efficiency. But he caught himself, reminding himself that people—whether they are students in a classroom or family at a dinner table—need empathy to thrive.

As weeks turned into months, Remigio noticed a shift in his interactions. He chose to listen deeply when Maria, a usually bubbly student, became withdrawn and silent. Instead of reprimanding her for falling grades, he invited her for a chat. Maria opened up about a turbulent situation at home that was affecting her concentration and self-esteem. Remigio felt like the walls he had built over the years crumbled.

He arranged for Maria to receive emotional support and adjusted her academic workload. Seeing Maria's turnaround was a eureka moment for Remigio, the ultimate validation of his empathic journey. And it didn't stop there. This newfound connectivity made the classroom environment more robust and harmonious, encouraging even the quieter students to engage in discussions and group activities.

The benefits of his transformation rippled into his personal life as well. Conversations with friends and loved ones became more substantial and fulfilling. His ability to navigate emotional under-currents improved dramatically, leading to stronger, healthier relationships.

So, what's the moral of Remigio's story? Sometimes, the best lessons a teacher can offer are the ones he learns himself. For Remigio, empathy became more than just a teaching tool—it became a way of life, enhancing not only his classroom but also enriching his personal interactions. He realized that the hearts and minds of his students were not compartments but two sides of the same coin, both deserving his attention.

In the end, Remigio learned that being an exceptional teacher meant more than just producing top-grade students; it meant nurturing well-rounded individuals. He wasn't just teaching equations and grammar; he was helping to shape the next generation of emotionally intelligent human beings. And for Remigio, that was the most rewarding lesson of all.

SIX

Step #6—Managing Relationships

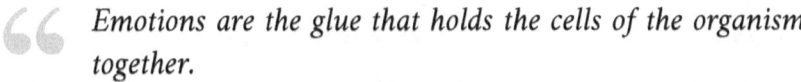

Emotions are the glue that holds the cells of the organism together.

Candace Pert

I n this fast-paced world we're living in, it's so easy to lose sight of the things that really matter. And let me tell you, the quality of our relationships is at the top of that list. We're talking about the friendships that lift you up, the love that fills your heart, and even those work connections that make your nine-to-five a bit more bearable. These relationships are our emotional backbone; they keep us standing tall when life tries to pull us down.

So, what's the secret sauce to a relationship that not only lasts but thrives? Well, we're going to dig deep into that. Communication, my friends, is your bread and butter. You've got to talk, listen, and, most importantly, understand each other. Now, don't underestimate the power of emotional intelligence. Recognizing your feelings and the feelings of those around you? That's golden.

But it doesn't stop there. A relationship is a two-way street. Both sides have to want to travel in the same direction. Whether it's your partner, your friend, or your coworker, it's all about working together toward common goals and celebrating each other's wins, big or small.

Nurturing Healthy Relationships

Let's talk about something we all yearn for: healthy relationships. Now, what makes a relationship healthy, you ask? First and foremost, it's built on a foundation of trust and honesty. That means no secrets, no shadiness, just pure, open communication. It's a place where both parties feel respected and appreciated, not just as part of a couple but as individuals, too.

When you're in a healthy relationship, both of you should feel secure enough to be your true selves. That's right—no masks, no pretenses. And let's not forget, in a true partnership, both parties share the responsibilities as well as the decisions. It's not a "you or me" situation; it's "us and we."

But here's the kicker: A healthy relationship is one without fear, intimidation, or retaliation. You should never feel like you're walking on eggshells, worried about the repercussions of speaking your truth. Instead, you should feel uplifted, supported, and empowered by your partner.

So, if you're asking yourself, "Is my relationship healthy?" Look for these signs, listen to your inner voice, and most importantly, honor your true self. It's the best gift you can give to yourself and to the relationship. Stay tuned; we're just scratching the surface. Up next, we delve deeper into the magic of maintaining this beautiful bond.

How to Nurture Relationships With Emotional Intelligence

Now that we've talked about what a healthy relationship looks like, let's delve into how to use your emotional intelligence to nurture these connections. You see, emotional intelligence isn't just a buzzword; it's a life skill, a superpower even. It's the key to making your relationships sing.

First things first, keep that communication open, honest, and clear. We all know how easy it is to let misunderstandings brew and fester. Open communication allows you to understand not only what's being said but also the emotional subtext behind it. That's right, it's not just about the words; it's about the feelings and intentions behind those words.

Disagreements are inevitable. But emotional intelligence teaches you to navigate those choppy waters. The goal is not to win an argument but to understand the other person's point of view. It's okay to disagree; it's not okay to dismiss. Address disagreements head-on, but always in a way that maintains both parties' dignity.

You need to create a safe space for emotional connection. In a world that often values tough exteriors, emotional intelligence allows you to be vulnerable and lets others feel safe doing the same with you. When people feel heard and understood, that's when emotional bonds strengthen.

Last but not least, practice empathy. Put yourself in their shoes, feel what they're feeling, and let them know you're right there with them. Not above, not below, just side by side.

So, there you have it. A blueprint for using emotional intelligence to nurture your relationships. Keep these practices in mind, make them part of your daily interactions, and watch how they transform not only your relationships but you as a person. Stick around because we've got more wisdom to share in the next chapter.

Conflict Resolution Strategies

Conflicts can be unsettling and disruptive, but often necessary for growth and transformation. So, let's talk about how to navigate through these storms with your relationships intact. Here are ten strategies to tackle conflicts with grace and wisdom.

- **Take a timeout:** We've all been there, getting heated in the moment and wanting to say the first thing that comes to mind. Resist that urge. Stepping away helps you avoid escalation and gives you the opportunity to breathe. During this time, think about what really matters to you in the situation and what you want to accomplish by addressing it. It's a moment of peace before going back to face the storm.
- **Listen, really listen:** It's so easy to interrupt and interject our own thoughts. But hold on a second, literally. When you actively listen, you are giving the other person the space to express themselves fully. This kind of full attention fosters mutual respect and helps you get to the root of the issue. Understanding is the first step toward resolution.
- **Speak your truth, but be kind:** Honesty is the best policy, but delivery is key. Being considerate in your speech doesn't mean watering down your feelings; it means addressing the situation in a respectful manner. Clearly articulate your concerns without blaming or shaming the other person. Your words are powerful; use them to build bridges, not walls.

- **Find common ground:** In any conflict, there's something that you both want—even if it's just a peaceful resolution. Identifying mutual goals can serve as a foundation for constructive dialogue. This shared understanding can help to humanize each party in the eyes of the other, turning opponents into partners working toward a solution.

- **Be open to compromise:** Being rigid in your viewpoints isn't going to get you anywhere. Openness to compromise shows maturity and a willingness to maintain the relationship. Consider alternative solutions that address both parties' concerns. This is a two-way street, and both need to feel satisfied with the outcome.

- **Choose the right time and place:** A calm environment can make all the difference. If tensions are already high, adding a stressful setting to the mix can be a recipe for disaster. Opt for a comfortable location where you can talk openly and freely. Timing and setting are more than just logistics; they set the stage for meaningful dialogue.

- **Stay present:** It's tempting to dredge up the past in a conflict, but this often does more harm than good. Focus on the issue currently on the table and how it can be resolved. Looking back distracts you from the problem at hand, and you risk muddying the waters with unrelated issues. Keep your eyes on the road ahead.

- **Be accountable:** It's not always easy to admit when you're wrong. But doing so is a sign of emotional maturity. Saying sorry can be a powerful gesture that rebuilds trust. It shows you value the relationship more than your ego. Accountability can turn a conflict into an opportunity for growth.

- **Seek third-party help:** Sometimes, the solution is not clear, and an outside perspective can help. A therapist or counselor can offer neutral insights that may reveal the underlying issues. But this isn't a sign of failure; it's a sign of commitment to resolving the conflict and improving the relationship.

- **Agree to disagree:** At times, you'll find that you're at an impasse. Acknowledging that it's okay to have differing opinions can be liberating. This doesn't mean giving up; it means recognizing the uniqueness of each individual. You can respect each other's viewpoints while still maintaining a strong relationship.

So, there you have it! These aren't just strategies; they're life lessons for navigating the complexity of human relationships. Next, we're going to delve even deeper into how to enrich your life through meaningful connections. Stick around; it's going to be enlightening!

Building Trust and Fostering Collaboration

Trust is a word that's packed with so much meaning, isn't it? Imagine for a moment your life without trust. You'd be wading through quicksand uncertain at every turn. Trust is like that invisible thread that weaves the fabric of our relationships, making them strong and resilient. It's not just about having someone's back; it's about knowing they have yours, too. When you trust, you give yourself permission to be your authentic self, and you create space for others to do the same.

Now, I want you to feel this in your core: When you have trust in a relationship, it's like sunshine on a cloudy day. You see, trust lights up the room—or the office, for that matter. It transforms working environments from places of skepticism and doubt to platforms for creativity, cooperation, and collective success. Trust is what makes the difference between a team and a community.

But let's talk about what happens when trust is missing from the equation: the side glances, the whispers, the doubts that eat away at your soul. A relationship without trust is like a car without gas —you're going nowhere fast. And that feeling of uncertainty? That's not just in your head; it's a fog that clouds everyone's judgment and halts progress.

You see, building trust isn't a "one-and-done" kind of deal. It's not a box you can just check off. Trust is a living, breathing entity that needs constant nourishment. Every word you speak, every action you take—they're all brushstrokes in the larger painting of trust. And when you invest in building trust, what you're really doing is investing in a better life for yourself and everyone around you.

How to Build Trust and Collaboration

If you're ready to transform your relationships, your teams, and even your communities, listen up. We're diving into some wisdom here that's not just going to change the game; it's going to change your life. Let's get into it!

First up, let's talk about honesty and direct communication. I'm sure you've heard the saying, "Honesty is the best policy." Well, it's not just a cute phrase; it's the cornerstone of trust. When you're open and transparent, you're not only showing respect to others, but you're also setting the stage for a relationship built on trust. If you say what you mean and mean what you say, you give others permission to do the same. And trust me, that's where the magic happens.

To implement this, begin by setting the tone for open dialogue. Maybe it's a regular team meeting where everyone gets to voice their opinions or concerns. Encourage everyone to be candid but respectful. Show that you value honesty by being the first to communicate openly, and make sure to listen when others follow suit. Trust builds one conversation at a time.

Now, I want you to feel this: Creative collaboration is not just a one-and-done concept—it's a lifeline for innovation. Create spaces and opportunities for your team to brainstorm, dream, and innovate together. Not only will this bring forth fantastic ideas, but it will also help people feel invested in the mission, knowing that their input is valued. Collaborating creatively breaks down barriers and creates a fertile ground for trust to grow.

So, how do we make this real? Start by organizing brainstorming sessions or workshops focused on creative problem-solving. Make sure everyone knows their ideas are welcome, no matter how "out there" they may seem. And let the creative juices flow without judgment—sometimes, the craziest ideas are the seeds for something transformative. Remember, collaboration is a two-way street, so jump in and get your hands dirty, too.

Let's move on to empowering your team to be self-organized. Friends, if you want people to step up, you've got to let them stand up. Give your team the freedom to make decisions, to solve problems, and to truly own their roles. This doesn't mean abandoning structure; it means enabling autonomy within a framework. When people feel empowered, they take on challenges with gusto—and let me tell you, trust thrives in this kind of environment.

Ready to put this into action? It's all about balance. Provide your team with the tools and resources they need, and then step back. Let them take the wheel while you're there as a guide, not as a micromanager. Weekly check-ins can be a great way to stay connected without being overbearing. Trust that they will come to you if they hit a roadblock that they can't navigate around.

Now, here's something that often gets overlooked: clarity in roles and responsibilities. A lot of the time, mistrust comes from misunderstandings and confusion. So do everyone a favor and keep those roles crystal clear. Make sure everybody knows not just what they're doing, but why they're doing it. Clarity reduces friction, and when friction is low, trust can glide right in.

To bring this into your life, take time to clearly outline everyone's roles and responsibilities. Write it down, discuss it, and make sure everyone is on the same page. If possible, involve team members in the process of defining their roles—it leads to greater ownership and understanding. Regularly revisit these roles, especially during times of change, to ensure everyone remains clear on their contributions.

And last but certainly not least, make feedback part of your team culture. Open, constructive feedback is like the water and sunshine for the garden of trust—it helps it grow and flourish. Make it okay to give and receive feedback, both positive and critical. But remember, feedback is not just about pointing out the gaps; it's also about celebrating the wins, big and small.

How do we make this a reality? Create safe spaces for feedback, perhaps through one-on-one meetings or even anonymous suggestion boxes for those who prefer it. Make it a point to ask for feedback during team meetings, showing that it's not only okay but encouraged. And when you give feedback, make it specific, constructive, and immediate. It's not just about what's not working; celebrate the wins, too, and soon enough, a feedback culture will take root.

Wrapping Up

Let's circle back to our chapter hook by Candace Pert: "Emotions are the glue that holds the cells of the organism together." Just like cells, the members of a team are held together by the glue of trust, emotional intelligence, and effective communication. What we've learned today goes beyond strategy or management lingo; it digs deep into the human elements that can make or break a team's cohesion.

Quick recap:

- Open and honest communication: The cornerstone of trust and collaboration.
- Creative collaboration: A playground for the mind that invites innovation.
- Empowerment: Let your team own their tasks, but provide a safety net.
- Clarity of roles: Keep everyone on the same page to avoid conflicts.
- Feedback culture: A must for growth and continuous improvement.

As we close this chapter, remember that managing relationships isn't just about getting along. It's about nurturing an environment where every team member can thrive, both individually and collectively. So, what's the next vital step on this journey? Well, let's just say you'll want to stick around because we're about to dig into the power of emotional resilience—your secret weapon for life's most challenging moments. Don't miss it!

Case Study: Lucy

I had this friend in college, Lucy, and the friendship we formed seemed almost serendipitous. We had the same major, ran into each other in three separate classes, and it felt like destiny was practically shouting, "Hey, you two should be friends!" So, we hung out, studied for exams together, and got to know each other's hopes, fears, and, of course, the kinds of food we each swore by during final exam season (mine was pizza; hers was Chinese takeout).

But friendships, much like anything valuable in life, aren't just about the good times. No matter how close you get to someone, there will be moments where you don't see eye-to-eye. For Lucy and me, disagreements came up every now and then. I guess we were both strong-willed and opinionated, which is both a blessing and a curse. There were times when our disagreements seemed like they'd reach a breaking point. Yet we both knew deep down that maintaining our friendship mattered more than winning any argument. So, we made a pact to find healthier ways to deal with conflicts.

One of the most memorable examples was a summer road trip we'd been looking forward to. Now, I was all for soaking in the vibes of small-town diners and sleeping in motels with questionable linens. Lucy, on the other hand, was dreaming of pitching a tent under the stars and hiking up rocky trails. It seemed like we were at an impasse. But instead of canceling the trip or jeopardizing our friendship, we each sat down and made a list of non-negotiables and things we were willing to compromise on. By the end of it, we had a roadmap of cities, campsites, diners, and trails that accommodated both our interests.

Trust is another invisible yet sturdy pillar that held up our friendship. I think we both understood early on that to make our friendship work, we needed more than just shared interests and free weekends. Trust was the currency of our friendship economy, and we built it through unfiltered conversations and being there for each other, no questions asked.

During group projects or planning events together, trust was the undercurrent that made everything run smoothly. We divided tasks based on our strengths, kept each other in the loop, and, most importantly, created a safe space to express our opinions and feedback. And you know what? It was this cycle of trust, collaboration, and open dialogue that not only made our projects successful but also fortified our friendship.

So, if I've learned anything from my years of friendship with Lucy, it's that relationships, whether they are platonic or romantic, are an ongoing project. They need a certain level of emotional finesse. That means being able to navigate conflicts without damaging the relationship, committing to truly understanding the other person, and creating a safety net of trust that catches you both when things get tough.

Take a moment to reflect on your relationships. Are there recurring conflicts that need a different approach? How open and safe is the communication? What steps can you take to foster a greater sense of trust? Because remember, relationships aren't just a key part of life; they are life itself. And understanding how to manage them is a journey well worth the effort.

Case Study: Lucas

Remember Remigio from the last chapter? Let's see how his mastery of EI impacted his student, Lucas. When Remigio first encountered Lucas, a student in his high school English class, he found himself grappling with frustration and a sense of helplessness. Lucas was known to be disruptive, his actions a loud echo in the hushed hallways of disciplinary action. Other teachers had seemingly written him off, a "troublemaker" stamped invisibly but indelibly on his forehead. Remigio himself had, at first, sighed in resignation, preparing himself for a year of constant disruptions.

But then something changed in Remigio. He began diving deep into the realm of emotional intelligence, learning the nuanced language of empathy, active listening, and effective communication. It was as if someone had handed him a new pair of glasses, bringing the world into sharp, compassionate focus.

Armed with this newfound perspective, he saw Lucas not as a classroom irritant but as a complex individual. He decided to toss the traditional disciplinary playbook and took a radically different approach.

After class one day, Remigio asked Lucas to stay back for a moment. Instead of launching into a lecture, he simply asked, "Hey, you've seemed a bit off lately. Everything okay?" Remigio had prepared himself for a dismissive shrug or a defensive snarl. But Lucas paused. In that silence, the walls of defiance seemed to waver and then crumble. What came out was a torrent of words— Lucas's parents were in the middle of a chaotic divorce, and he felt like he was teetering on the edge of an abyss.

In that moment, Remigio did something he might not have done before his emotional intelligence journey: he listened. Not just passively, but with active, intentional empathy. He didn't interrupt or offer any solutions. He let Lucas speak, only occasionally nodding or offering a quiet "I understand" to encourage him to continue. He also suggested Lucas consider talking to a school counselor, offering to facilitate that connection if it would make things easier.

As weeks turned into months, Lucas began to change. The rowdy interruptions ceased, replaced by tentative, then confident, participation. Remigio noticed that Lucas even started to help others in the class, offering to share his notes or explain a complex point. And as Lucas changed, so did the class dynamic. The students, once wary and distant, started to warm up to Lucas, embracing him as one of their own.

At the end of the school year, Remigio realized the true depth of the transformation. Lucas was not just another student he had "managed" to teach; he was a vivid testament to the life-altering power of emotional intelligence. It was a lesson that Remigio knew would shape the way he approached teaching—and life—for years to come. It wasn't just about academic achievements or maintaining discipline; it was about reaching into the tangled brush of human emotion and experience and finding a way to nurture the fragile blooms of potential waiting there. And that made all the difference.

SEVEN

Step #7—Applying Emotional Intelligence Professionally

 As much as 80% of adult 'success' comes from EQ.

Daniel Goleman

Now, if that doesn't grab your attention, I don't know what will. We've spent the last six chapters diving deep into the nuances of emotional intelligence and understanding its role in our personal lives. But let's not forget where we spend a massive chunk of our waking hours—our professional lives.

You see, EQ—or emotional intelligence—isn't just a personal affair. It's an office affair, a team affair, and yes, a success affair. This isn't about learning how to "win friends and influence people," although that's certainly a happy byproduct. No, this is about authentic engagement with your work and the people who make that work happen. It's about fostering a better understanding of yourself so that you can navigate the complexities of interpersonal relations in the workplace. It's about realizing your full potential as a leader, a team member, or even as the go-to person when anyone needs advice.

The goal for this final chapter is crystal clear. We're going to explore how mastering emotional intelligence can be a game-changer in your professional life. We're about to bring everything full circle and show you how to make EQ your secret weapon for professional success.

Leveraging Emotional Intelligence Professionally

You know how we often say that intelligence gets you through the door, but it's your people skills that build the house? Well, that's where EQ comes into play, especially in your career. Remember what Daniel Goleman said? "As much as 80% of adult 'success' comes from EQ." That's huge!

So, you've learned about EQ, but how do you actually put that knowledge to work in your daily grind? First things first, this isn't a once-and-done deal. Your EQ is like your career's emotional pulse—it's always there, always ticking. Think of it as your secret sauce in navigating the maze of office politics and team dynamics.

Going for a promotion or eyeing a leadership role? Your EQ is your ally. When the heat is on and everyone else is losing their cool, you're the one who stays steady. That's the kind of leader people can get behind.

But let's not just focus on the top of the ladder. EQ is just as important in creating meaningful connections with everyone from the mailroom to the boardroom. You're not just "networking"— you're building genuine relationships. This isn't just for the annual office party; it's your lifelong professional circle we're talking about.

What about when things shake up, like a merger or a shift in company strategy? A strong EQ means you can roll with the punches. You're not just surviving these changes; you're the one who's savvy enough to pivot and thrive.

In the end, EQ isn't just a nice-to-have; it's a need-to-have. It's not just about being a team player or a good listener, as important as those are. Your EQ helps you evolve, engage, and excel in your career in a way that sets you apart. So, if you're wondering how EQ fits into the professional picture—trust me, it's not just part of the frame; it's the whole darn painting.

Emotional Intelligence in Leadership and Teamwork

Do you know how some folks just seem to have that magical touch when it comes to leading a team or collaborating effectively? Chances are, they have a high EQ.

What does EQ mean for leadership and teamwork? For starters, it's the bedrock of effective communication. We're talking about way more than just exchanging pleasantries at the water cooler. Leaders with high EQ have this knack for really "getting" people. They read the room, sense underlying issues, and know when it's time to offer a word of encouragement—or when to back off. The result? A team that feels heard and valued. That's how you create a work environment where people aren't just clocking in and out; they're engaged and committed.

But let's go beyond that. High-EQ leaders aren't just motivators; they're also influencers. Think of the best boss you've ever had. They didn't just bark orders from a corner office, right? They inspired you. They understood what makes you tick and leveraged that to help you reach new heights. It's not about manipulation; it's about cultivating a sense of purpose and belonging. When a leader can create that kind of vibe, productivity isn't just a metric—it's a mission.

And here's another point: EQ is the fuel that keeps the collaborative engine running smoothly. You know how in every group project, there's always that one person who just can't play well with others? With a higher collective EQ, teams are more in sync, better at resolving conflicts, and, frankly, just a lot more fun to be a part of. It's not just about individual contributions; it's about how those contributions come together to create something bigger than the sum of its parts.

In short, a high EQ is important whether you're leading the charge or part of the rank and file. It's the skill that turns group efforts into group successes and maybe—just maybe—makes Monday mornings a bit more bearable.

Handling Workplace Stress and Pressure

We've all been there—Monday rolls around and it feels like the universe has decided to dump a whole load of stress onto your desk. Deadlines are looming, clients are demanding, and let's not even talk about the coffee machine being out of order. This is where the magic of EQ comes into play.

High-EQ individuals are not immune to stress; they just deal with it differently. When you've got a high EQ, you're more in tune with your emotions and how they're affecting your body. Feel that tension creeping into your shoulders? A rapid heartbeat or shallow breathing? Recognizing these physical cues is step one. It's like your body saying, "Hey, something's up. You might want to deal with this."

The next move is to get those emotions out of the driver's seat. It doesn't mean dismissing or suppressing them; it means acknowledging them without letting them dictate your actions. This is easier said than done, of course. However, taking a few deep breaths, stepping away from your desk, or doing some quick mindfulness exercises can serve as emotional circuit breakers, helping you to think more clearly and make more rational decisions.

And here's another tip: leverage the power of empathy. We often think of empathy as something we extend to others, but what about extending it to ourselves? Instead of beating yourself up for feeling stressed, acknowledge that it's okay to feel this way. Self-compassion can actually be a game changer in how you cope with stress.

But let's not forget about your interactions with others. Work is a team sport, and your EQ can make you a better player. If you're sensing tension in the room or picking up on the stress levels of your colleagues, a high EQ allows you to address it in a productive way. Maybe it's offering a word of encouragement, lending a listening ear, or even taking the lead on a group meditation session. After all, a stress-free team is often a more productive one.

In a nutshell, having a high EQ doesn't make workplace challenges go away. But it gives you the tools to tackle them head-on, keeping your cool while you do. And who knows, you might just become the person everyone wants to be around when the going gets tough.

You've come this far, soaking up all this wisdom on EQ and its impact on your career. But let's get down to brass tacks—how do you actually take all this theory and put it into practice? Here are some concrete steps to weave emotional intelligence into your daily professional life.

Practical Steps to Integrate Emotional Intelligence Into Your Professional Life

Step 1: Self-Assessment

The journey starts with you. Take a few minutes every week to reflect on your emotional responses and behavior at work. Did you handle that tense meeting as well as you could have? Were you really present during that client interaction? This isn't about being hard on yourself; it's about understanding where you're at so you can get to where you want to be.

Step 2: Active Listening

We often think we're great listeners, but most of us are just waiting for our turn to speak. The next time you're in a conversation at work, challenge yourself to really focus on the other person. Hear them out completely before formulating your response. You'd be surprised how much this simple change can improve your inter-personal interactions.

Step 3: Empathize, Don't Sympathize

Sympathy is saying, "I'm sorry you're feeling this way." Empathy is putting yourself in their shoes and understanding why they feel that way. The latter is a far more powerful tool in the workplace because it fosters genuine connections.

Step 4: Manage Your Triggers

Identify what sets you off at work. Is it a last-minute deadline? A particular coworker? Knowing your triggers can help you prepare a more emotionally intelligent response. Or, at the very least, give you a few seconds to take those deep breaths we talked about earlier.

Step 5: Seek Feedback

If you want to get better at anything, you've got to be willing to hear how you're doing. Seek out constructive criticism from colleagues and mentors who you respect and admire. And remember, it's not a critique of you as a person—it's an avenue for growth.

Step 6: Foster Team EQ

Believe it or not, emotional intelligence can be contagious. If you're putting all these practices into play, chances are your colleagues will notice and might even get inspired to do the same. Keep an eye out for ways to foster EQ within your team, whether it's through team-building activities, open dialogues about workplace culture, or just being a good role model.

Step 7: Keep Learning

The landscape of emotional intelligence is ever-evolving. Keep up with new studies and articles or even take some online courses to stay on top of your EQ game.

By following these steps, you're not just talking the talk; you're walking the walk. The beautiful thing about emotional intelligence is that it's not a destination but a journey—one that can enrich not just your career but your life as a whole.

So go ahead, roll up those sleeves, and start integrating these steps into your professional life. You've got this.

Wrapping Up

So, let's circle back to where we started this conversation: "As much as 80% of adult 'success' comes from EQ," Daniel Goleman said. If you've read through this chapter, it's clear that emotional intelligence isn't just a feel-good buzzword; it's the bedrock upon which your career success is built. And if 80% of your success depends on it, then it's worth every ounce of effort you put into it, isn't it?

What you've learned:

- the direct impact of EQ on your career trajectory and why it can't be ignored
- how emotional intelligence benefits leadership skills and team dynamics
- effective ways to manage workplace stress through a higher EQ
- practical steps you can start taking today to weave emotional intelligence into your professional life

Take this knowledge and these tools with you as you go about your daily grind. Recognize your emotional responses, connect genuinely with others, manage your triggers, and most of all, keep growing. Because when you grow emotionally, your professional life will follow suit.

And there it is, the secret sauce to not just surviving in your career, but truly thriving. So go ahead, make Daniel Goleman proud—after all, 80% of your success is calling.

Case Study: Andre

Have you ever stopped to wonder why some people just seem to shine at work? I'm not talking about the Ivy League resumes or the hyper-organized project planners. I'm talking about the folks who bring something intangible to the table, who everyone wants on their team. I learned this lesson from my colleague, Andre, whose secret weapon isn't a fancy degree or technical wizardry; it's emotional intelligence.

Let's break it down a bit, shall we? Emotional intelligence isn't just an esoteric concept—it's the quiet pulse of a thriving workplace. Imagine walking into a team meeting where people don't just clock in their opinions like they're punching a time card. Instead, they're fully present, led by Andre, who seems to have an almost sixth sense of the room's emotional temperature. He knows when Sarah is uneasy about a deadline or when Mark isn't speaking up because he feels unheard. By addressing these undercurrents, Andre doesn't just manage a team; he nurtures a community.

We often overlook the "soft skills" like empathy or active listening, dismissing them as less crucial than hard skills. But Andre's career trajectory begs to differ. Every year, like clockwork, he's been climbing that corporate ladder. Not by showing off his spreadsheet skills, although I'm sure they're excellent, but by showcasing something far more important: his humanity.

What's really awe-inspiring is how Andre manages stress. High-stake client meetings, tight deadlines—you name it, he's faced it, and always with remarkable grace. We've all been there, right? The pit in your stomach, the shaky hands. But Andre has a way of transforming that nervous energy into something constructive. He practices deep breathing, he shifts his mindset, but most importantly, he shares these tools with us. The impact on team morale? Immeasurable.

It's not a one-and-done deal for Andre; he's committed to growing his emotional intelligence. He reads, takes courses, and even seeks mentorship. This isn't about navel-gazing; it's about being coura-geously self-aware. Andre knows his triggers, he understands his boundaries, and he brings this self-knowledge into every interaction.

Skills like coding or finance might get you in the door, but it's emotional intelligence that takes you to the corner office. So, let's pause for some real talk. How emotionally intelligent are you at work? Are you a leader who can sit with discomfort, who can genuinely listen and show up wholeheartedly for your team? And how are you nurturing these qualities in your own professional life?

Case Study: Elliot

When Elliot, a rising star at a prestigious marketing firm, was handed the reins of a critical project, everyone expected results as slick and polished as his presentations. But as weeks went by, his team seemed disjointed, their efforts half-hearted. Elliot was baffled; he was an excellent communicator, had top-notch analytical skills, and always aced his performance reviews. So why were things falling apart now?

Around the same time, Elliot stumbled upon a book about emotional intelligence as part of a leadership development course he was taking. Intrigued, he turned to Chapter 7: Applying Emotional Intelligence Professionally. As he read through the concepts of empathetic leadership, effective communication, and the value of emotional self-awareness in the workplace, Elliot had an epiphany.

He began to reassess his leadership style. In meetings, he started focusing on not just the "what" but also the "how." Were his team members engaged? Were they reluctant to voice their opinions? He also realized he had never genuinely asked for feedback; it was always about the deadlines and the deliverables.

Emboldened by his newfound knowledge, Elliot decided to make some changes. He initiated one-on-one check-ins with team members, not to discuss the project, but to understand them better. What were their career goals? What drove them? What were their challenges? The conversations were awkward at first, but as Elliot showed genuine interest, the barriers began to come down.

Taking cues from the chapter, he also implemented active listening in group settings. Gone were the days when he would multitask during team meetings. He paid full attention, encouraged others to speak, and made sure to acknowledge their points before offering his views.

EIGHT

Emotional Intelligence in the Digital Age

I n our rapidly evolving digital age, the landscape of emotional intelligence (EQ) has experienced a seismic shift. While the core principles of understanding and managing emotions remain steadfast, the avenues for expression, interaction, and interpretation have expanded exponentially. No longer confined to face-to-face encounters or even voice-to-voice telephone calls, our emotional lives have moved into a realm that includes text messages, social media posts, video conferencing, and an ever-growing list of digital platforms. Each of these mediums presents its own unique challenges and opportunities for emotional expression and understanding.

The traditional cues we rely on to gauge someone's emotions—such as facial expressions, tone of voice, and body language—often vanish or become distorted in digital communication. Something as simple as a poorly chosen emoji or an email that seems curt can miscommunicate our intentions or misinterpret someone else's. The risks are not just misunderstandings but also the erosion of emotional connection and the fostering of negativity. However, digital platforms also offer new ways to connect emotionally and understand each other—if we adapt our emotional intelligence skills to this new terrain.

That's why the significance of adapting our EQ skills for virtual interactions cannot be overstated. In a world where remote work is increasingly the norm and friendships can flourish online, understanding how to express empathy, build rapport, and read emotional cues in a digital format is not just useful—it's essential. It's about more than saving face; it's about making sure we're accurately conveying who we are and what we feel in a medium that can easily muddle those messages. Whether you're navigating emotional undercurrents in a work Slack channel or trying to offer genuine support to a friend via text, honing your digital-age EQ skills can make the difference between meaningful connection and frustrating miscommunication.

This chapter will equip you with the insights and tools you need to successfully navigate the complex emotional landscape of today's digital age. From understanding the subtleties of virtual communication to building authentic connections online, we'll explore how to apply and adapt the timeless principles of emotional intelligence in this uncharted territory.

The Double-Edged Sword of Technology

Technology is our society's most prominent double-edged sword, particularly when it comes to emotional connections. On the one hand, it's never been easier to reach out, share, and connect with people from all walks of life across every imaginable distance. With a swipe and a click, we can share life updates with hundreds of friends and family members or even create new relationships based on shared interests and goals. But let's not forget the other edge of that sword, where digital interaction can often dilute emotional nuance, leading to misunderstandings or, worse, the breakdown of relationships.

Let's consider the story of Sarah and Maria, two close friends since college. Both women are avid users of social media, but their experiences have been markedly different. Sarah recently moved across the country and has been using video calls and messaging apps to maintain her friendships, including her relationship with Maria. She often shares pictures of her new city, virtually inviting Maria into her life. The technology has facilitated a level of connection that would have been unthinkable in an era of expensive long-distance phone calls and snail mail. In this case, technology acts as a bridge, making a geographically distant friendship feel emotionally close.

Maria, on the other hand, has had a different journey. She uses social media platforms heavily but finds herself feeling increasingly isolated. The "like" and "heart" buttons feel insufficient for expressing her feelings, and she's had her share of disagreements escalate unnecessarily due to the limitations of text-based communication. She misses the days when she could see Sarah's expressions, hear the tone of her voice, or simply enjoy a moment of silence together without it feeling awkward. For Maria, technology often feels like a barrier rather than a bridge, a constant reminder of the physical and emotional distance that now separates her from her friend.

Then there's Mark, a project manager who has seen the pros and cons of technology play out in the professional realm. Mark manages a remote team and has found tools like Slack invaluable for quick updates and immediate feedback, fostering a sense of team cohesion and collective achievement. Yet, he's also noticed that heavy reliance on digital communication means he's missing out on the emotional cues that naturally occur in a traditional office setting—those off-hand comments before a meeting starts or the subtle facial expressions that indicate confusion, disagreement, or inspiration. Mark finds himself setting up regular video conferences just to "take the pulse" of the team, an extra step that wouldn't be necessary in a physical workspace.

In these stories, the common thread is the need for balance and adaptation. Technology offers incredible tools for emotional connection, but these tools are only as effective as our ability to adapt our emotional intelligence to new forms of communication. The key is not to reject technology but to wield it wisely, understanding its limitations while making the most of its extraordinary capabilities for connection. So, as we continue to text, tweet, post, and video call, let's make sure we're also continuing to listen, understand, and connect—in every sense of those words.

Virtual Communication: Beyond Words

In the era of screens and virtual communication, where does emotional nuance fit in? We might not have the luxury of reading facial expressions or interpreting vocal inflections when we're texting or emailing, but that doesn't mean emotional intelligence has no place in digital interactions. It's all about understanding the new cues—tone, timing, and the choice of communication medium—along with a host of digital markers like emojis that are designed to convey emotion.

Let's start with tone. In face-to-face conversations, tone can carry more weight than the words themselves. But when you're typing, how do you convey tone? Punctuation becomes your best friend. Exclamation points can show excitement or urgency; ellipses can indicate hesitation or incomplete thoughts; and a well-placed "haha" can break tension just like a chuckle in person. These tiny markers can help you convey sarcasm, surprise, and everything in between.

Now, what about timing? In digital communication, *when* you say something can be just as important as what you're saying. Sending an urgent email late at night or during the weekend might send the message that you lack boundaries or don't respect the other person's time. On the other hand, timely responses can convey attentiveness and professionalism. In a digital world, where everyone is reachable at all hours, knowing when to reach out matters.

Your choice of communication medium also speaks volumes. In professional settings, an email is often more appropriate than a text, signaling a level of formality and consideration. Among friends, a video call might convey the importance of the conversation you want to have, suggesting it deserves more than a quick text exchange. Being mindful of how your choice of medium sets the tone for the conversation is a crucial part of emotional intelligence in the digital age.

But what about those cute emojis? Far from being frivolous, they've become essential tools for adding emotional context to digital communication. A smiling face can turn a blunt message into a friendly nudge, and a heart can convey warmth and sincerity. Emojis can also cross language barriers, offering a universal method of expressing emotions, approval, or concern. But remember: not all emojis are created equal in all contexts. What works in a text to a friend may not be appropriate in a professional email.

So, while we can't entirely replicate the richness of face-to-face communication in the digital realm, we're far from helpless. By paying attention to these new markers and cues—tone, timing, medium, and even emojis—we can express our emotional intelligence in ways that transcend words. We might be behind screens, but we're still human, after all, and the need for meaningful emotional connection remains a constant.

The Perils of Anonymity

Anonymity in the digital age can be both liberating and unsettling. On the one hand, it offers us the freedom to express ourselves without immediate judgment; on the other, it can erode the natural empathetic connections that form through face-to-face interactions. The veil of anonymity can significantly impact emotional intelligence and understanding, often exacerbating miscommunications and enabling less considerate behavior.

The power and immediacy of online communication sometimes make us forget the real human beings on the other end. Take, for instance, the comments section on social media platforms or articles. Discussions can quickly spiral into heated, vitriolic exchanges, with participants showing little regard for the emotional impact of their words. This lack of empathetic connection is often exacerbated by the absence of immediate physical cues like facial expressions and voice tone.

Even in semi-anonymous spaces, such as workplace chat applications, where everyone knows each other but lacks the nuances provided by in-person interaction, misunderstandings can thrive. Without the immediate feedback that comes from facial expressions and vocal tones, messages can easily be misconstrued, creating emotional tension and confusion that can linger.

So, how do we navigate these challenges? Here are some practical tips for maintaining empathy in anonymous or semi-anonymous digital spaces:

- **Pause before you post:** Before hitting "send," take a moment to reread your message. Would you say this to the person's face? If not, you might want to reconsider your words.
- **Humanize the digital:** Remind yourself that behind every username or email address is a real person with feelings and experiences. This perspective can help foster more thoughtful and empathetic interactions.
- **Ask for clarification:** If a message's tone or intent is unclear, don't hesitate to ask for more context. A simple "Could you clarify what you meant by that?" can resolve a lot of misunderstandings.
- **Be explicit about your emotions:** Text-based conversations lack the emotional nuance of face-to-face interactions. If a subject matter is emotionally charged, consider explicitly stating how you feel. For example, "I'm concerned about..." or "That actually makes me really happy."
- **Switch to video or voice:** For important conversations where emotional nuance is crucial, consider switching to a voice or video call. These formats bring back some of the missing context that text alone can't provide.
- **Establish ground rules:** If you're part of a regular online community, whether it's a Slack channel at work or a hobbyist forum, establishing guidelines for respectful interaction can set the tone for more empathetic communication.

By actively employing these strategies, you can help bridge the emotional and empathetic gaps that often accompany digital communication. The aim is not to eliminate the benefits of digital and anonymous interactions but to bring a level of emotional intelligence and understanding that ensures these interactions are as meaningful and respectful as they can be.

Summing Up: Key Takeaways and Their Applications

As we navigate the complex world of digital communication, it's clear that maintaining a high level of emotional intelligence (EQ) is more important than ever. The anonymity or semi-anonymity in online spaces can be a double-edged sword, providing both freedom and potential pitfalls when it comes to empathetic interaction.

Key Takeaways

- **Anonymity affects empathy:** The absence of facial cues and immediate feedback can make it easier to disengage from the emotional reality of interactions, leading to misunderstandings and sometimes, outright hostility.
- **Pause and reflect:** Before posting something online, consider the emotional weight and potential impact of your words. If you wouldn't say it face-to-face, perhaps reconsider.
- **Human element:** Always remember that behind each screen is a real person with their own feelings, beliefs, and experiences.
- **Seek clarification:** If you're unsure about the emotional tone of a digital interaction, don't hesitate to ask for clarification.
- **Be transparent about emotions:** In text-based communication, it's often useful to be explicit about how you're feeling to prevent misunderstandings.
- **Utilize multiple mediums:** For emotionally charged or important discussions, consider switching to voice or

video calls to add back the missing layers of emotional nuance.

Applications

The application of these takeaways is not confined to any specific platform or setting. Whether it's a work-related chat application, a social media platform, or an online discussion forum, these principles can be universally applied to improve the quality of digital interactions.

Keep Evolving Your EQ

The landscape of digital communication is continually evolving, and with it, the challenges and opportunities for empathetic interaction also change. As we move further into this digital age, it's crucial to make a conscious effort to continue developing your emotional intelligence skills. Consider this not just a one-off effort, but a journey—one that can bring richer, more meaningful interactions both online and off.

So, keep learning, adapting, and applying these insights. The digital age may offer its set of challenges to emotional understanding, but it also provides a unique platform to practice and improve our empathetic skills. Let's make the most of it.

A Chance to Pay It Forward

As you step forward into the wonderful chapter awaiting you, take a moment to hold the door open for someone else.

Simply by sharing your honest opinion of this book and a little about your own journey, you'll show new readers where they can find all the guidance they need to take control of their future.

YOUR OPINION MATTERS!
LEAVE A REVIEW TO HELP
OTHERS JUST LIKE YOU

Thank you so much for your support. We're all on our own journeys, but every ounce of help we can share makes a huge difference.

Scan the QR code to leave a review on Amazon!

Conclusion

So, there you have it. We've turned over every stone and explored the hidden corners of emotional intelligence, and hopefully, you've seen just how transformative this thing called EQ can be. It's not just a professional skill; it's a life skill. It's not just about how you manage a team at work; it's about how you manage your relationships, your family, and, yes, even yourself.

Remember the stories we read on this journey? Their successes were not flukes. They invested in their emotional intelligence and turned it into real, tangible change in their professional and personal lives. If they can do it, believe me, so can you. This isn't fiction; it's reality. Your reality. A reality where emotional intelligence is not a footnote but a headline in your life's story.

So, here's my call to action for you: Don't just let these pages gather dust. Make this book a lived experience. Let the lessons marinate, practice them daily, and watch as you become an agent of change—not just in your life but in the lives of those around you. This book is more than just words; it's a catalyst. By incorporating the wisdom here into your own life, you're not just elevating your game; you're elevating the game for everyone around you.

If you've found even a sliver of enlightenment, self-growth, or newfound understanding through this book, don't keep it to yourself. Leaving a review isn't just about praising the book; it's about creating a ripple effect of emotional intelligence. When you share what you've learned, you empower others to discover these truths for themselves. Think of it as passing the torch of enlightenment because when one person rises, we all rise.

I want you to take this as your marching order: Go live your life armed with a nuanced understanding of your emotions and those of others. Go live a life where you're not just surviving, but thriving. Become the architect of your own future, the curator of your relationships, and the CEO of your destiny. The future is not set in stone; it's molded by the choices we make, the people we impact, and the emotional wisdom we wield.

And always, always remember: This is just the beginning, not the finale. The beauty of emotional intelligence is that it grows and deepens with time and practice. Your best is not behind you; it's ahead, waiting for you to seize it. You've got this, and the best is still unfolding. So go ahead and lean into the messy, beautiful, and profoundly human journey of life. Your best chapters are yet to be written, and I can't wait to see where your story goes.

DON'T FORGET TO GRAB YOUR COPY OF
THE FREE SELF-REFLECTION WORKBOOK!

By finishing this book, you're already *off to a great start* in kicking off your journey towards mastering emotional intelligence.

If you haven't downloaded it yet, *don't miss out* on the FREE Self-Reflection Workbook!

As a way of saying thank you for your purchase, I am offering you a free copy this companion Self-Reflection Workbook. This workbook accompanies the lessons taught in *Chapter 2*, as a hands-on guide to prioritizing you!

It's more than just a workbook; it's a part of your personal journey, emphasizing the skills you need to master emotional intelligence with ease.

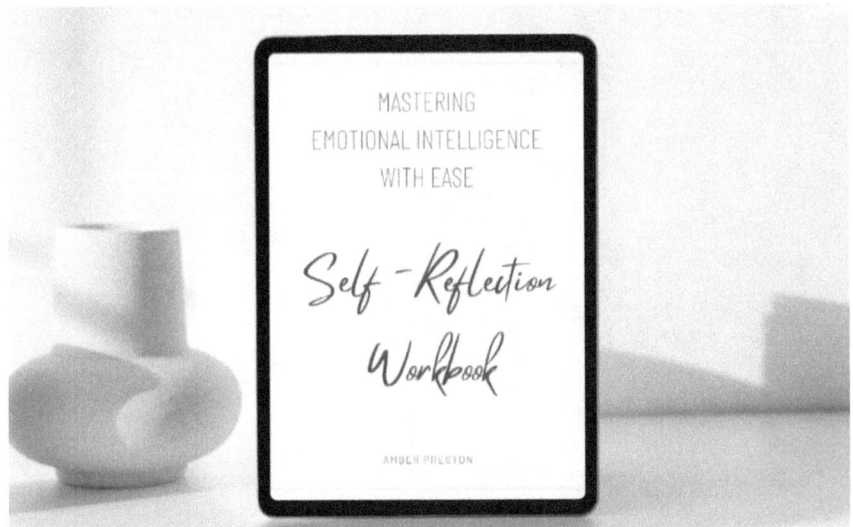

To get the free workbook, <u>click here</u> or scan the QR code below with your mobile phone!

References

Are you emotionally intelligent? Here's how to tell. (n.d.). Cornerstone University. https://www.cornerstone.edu/blog-post/are-you-emotionally-intelligent-heres-how-to-tell/

Betz, M. (2022, September 14). *What is self-awareness, and why is it important?* BetterUp. https://www.betterup.com/blog/what-is-self-awareness

Cherry, K. (2023, March 10). *What is self-Awareness?* Verywell Mind. https://www.verywellmind.com/what-is-self-awareness-2795023

Cherry, K. (2023, May 2). *How emotionally intelligent are you?* (n.d.). Verywell Mind. https://www.verywellmind.com/what-is-emotional-intelligence-2795423#:

Day, D. (n.d.). *Emotional intelligence quotes.* Sources of Insight. https://sourcesofinsight.com/emotional-intelligence-quotes/

Dumasio, A. (n.d.). *Emotional intelligence quotes.* Sources of Insight. https://sourcesofinsight.com/emotional-intelligence-quotes/

Emotional intelligence toolkit (n.d.). Helpguide. https://www.helpguide.org/articles/mental-health/emotional-intelligence-toolkit.htm#:

Eurich, T. (2018). *What self-awareness really Is (and how to cultivate it).* Harvard Business Review; hbr.org. https://hbr.org/2018/01/what-self-awareness-really-is-and-how-to-cultivate-it

Fort Newton, J. (n.d.). *Emotional intelligence quotes.* Sources of Insight. https://sourcesofinsight.com/emotional-intelligence-quotes/

Fritz, J., de Graaff, A. M., Caisley, H., van Harmelen, A.-L., & Wilkinson, P. O. (2018). A systematic review of amenable resilience factors that moderate and/or mediate the relationship between childhood adversity and mental health in young people. *Frontiers in Psychiatry, 9.* https://doi.org/10.3389/fpsyt.2018.00230

Goleman, D. (2021). *What is emotional self-awareness?* Kornferry. https://www.kornferry.com/insights/this-week-in-leadership/what-is-emotional-self-awareness

Jenson, E. (n.d.) *Emotional intelligence quotes.* Source of Insight. https://sourceofinsight.com/emotional-intelligence-quotes/

Mental Health America. (2023). *What is emotional intelligence and how does it apply to the workplace?* Mental Health America. https://mhanational.org/what-emotional-intelligence-and-how-does-it-apply-workplace

Meier, J. D. "Emotional Intelligence Quotes to Help You Master Your Emotions."

Last modified August 3, 2013. https://sourcesofinsight.com/emotional-intelli gence-quotes/.

Miller, K. (2020, March 13). *Building self-awareness: 16 activities and tools for meaningful change.* PositivePsychology.com. https://positivepsychology.com/build ing-self-awareness-activities/

Pert, C. (n.d.). *Emotional intelligence quotes.* Sources of Insight. https://sourcesofin sight.com/emotional-intelligence-quotes/

Rosenberg, M. (n.d.). *Emotional intelligence quotes.* Sources of Insight. https://source sofinsight.com/emotional-intelligence-quotes/

Schultz, M. (2019, September 18). *How do you build rapport with customers?* RAIN Group Sales Training. https://www.rainsalestraining.com/blog/how-do-you-build-rapport-with-customers#:

Schwantes, M. (2021, June 3). *Here's how to tell within 5 Minutes if someone has high emotional intelligence: skills that anyone can master with practice.* Inc. https://www. inc.com/marcel-schwantes/emotional-intelligence-how-to-tell.html#:

Wallbridge, A. (2023, February 27). *The importance Of self-awareness in emotional intelligence.* TSW Training. https://www.tsw.co.uk/blog/leadership-and-manage ment/self-awareness-in-emotional-intelligence/#:

Building Mental Toughness

7 PRACTICAL STEPS TO DEVELOP THE BEST
MINDSET FOR PEAK PERFORMANCE—
IMPROVE SELF-DISCIPLINE, BOOST
CONFIDENCE, STOP OVERTHINKING

Introduction

Life has a way of throwing curveballs when we least expect it. One moment, everything seems to be going smoothly—you're coasting along, handling your responsibilities, enjoying time with friends and family. The next moment, bam! A sudden challenge blindsides you, whether it's a strained relationship, a financial setback, or a personal loss. In times like these, you desperately yearn for an inner resilience that could help you bounce back. Instead, you feel emotionally brittle, like a thin sheet of ice that might crack at the slightest provocation.

This feeling of fragility often leaves you spinning in an endless loop of anxiety and self-doubt. You berate yourself for not being "tough enough"—strong enough to handle adversity with some semblance of grace. If only you could develop a thicker emotional hide, you tell yourself, you wouldn't crumble at every obstacle. So you try to suppress your difficult emotions through work, social media, or yet another Netflix binge. But the discontent lingers—a splinter in your mind.

If this experience resonates with you, you're not alone. We all want to believe we can muscle through challenges with stoic grit like some movie superhero. But real mental strength isn't about acting tough; it's about building emotional resilience through self-awareness and adaptability. Without understanding the root of our feelings and developing healthy coping mechanisms, any façade of toughness will eventually crack.

This book holds the keys to cultivating authentic, long-lasting mental strength accessible to anyone willing to do the soul-searching work. In *Building Mental Toughness*, I provide a 7-step training program for building mental muscle—not just surviving life's curveballs but thriving because of them. Through relatable storytelling and gentle guidance, you uncover how to

- rewire habitual thought patterns causing anxiety and overthinking
- develop confidence through vulnerability and self-compassion
- establish emotional boundaries for improved self-worth
- cultivate optimism and positivity whatever life brings

And so much more! Unlike restrictive one-size-fits-all solutions, the book offers tailored techniques for people across backgrounds and temperaments. You discover a versatility that enables you not just to power through challenges but grow because of them.

So, what's the catalyst for picking up this book? Well, ask yourself:

Do I tend to crumble when faced with obstacles, great and small?

Does adversity often plunge me into a pit of panic and gloom?

Would I like to handle life's curveballs with more emotional agility?

If you answered yes, then this book likely landed in your hands for a reason. Perhaps you're tired of living at the mercy of external ups and downs. Or maybe you want mental resilience not just for yourself but to model for your children. Whatever the catalyst, know that investing in this journey will provide dividends for years to come.

By reading this book, you're not just developing grit; you're reinventing life on your own terms. You discover lasting techniques to handle uncertainty, heal from hardship, and boldly pursue your aspirations. Instead of hiding your sensitivity, you leverage it for personal transformation.

Imagine showing up for your challenges with unflinching courage and optimism. Envision bouncing back from failures with renewed passion. Consider how self-trust and confidence could ripple through all areas of your life.

This all begins with the first step detailed in "Chapter 2: Stop Overthinking in its Tracks." Along the way, I will guide you with compassionate firmness—as the coach who believes in you more than you believe in yourself. Each carefully designed chapter concludes with inspiring real-world stories, reinforcing that change is truly possible.

If empowering yourself with unassailable mental strength sounds appealing, then join me on this life-changing journey of self-discovery and growth. This book builds upon the concepts introduced in *Mastering Emotional Intelligence With Ease*, providing additional insights and strategies to help you navigate life's challenges. However, even if you haven't read the previous book, you'll find valuable information and guidance within these pages. With the roadmap you'll soon find, adversity only makes you sharper, distress deepens your wisdom, and the obstacles once weighing you down have become catalysts for positive transformation. The life you've always imagined is closer than you think.

ONE

Understanding Mental Toughness

> *It's your reaction to adversity, not adversity itself that determines how your life's story will develop.*
>
> Dieter F. Uchtdorf

Life has a peculiar way of testing our mettle when we least expect it. Without warning, an unexpected challenge drops into our lap, and suddenly, we find ourselves face-to-face with adversity. Perhaps you've lost a job, ended a relationship, dealt with grief, or faced discrimination. In these turbulent times, you desperately wish you had nerves of steel and unshakable composure. But instead, you discover you're emotionally fragile—stressed, doubtful, and overwhelmed.

If this experience resonates with you, take comfort in knowing you're not alone. We all hope we'd face our firewalk unflinchingly, but the truth is, adversity often catches us off-guard, revealing our emotional brittleness. What if I told you there was another way?

Beyond just surviving life's curveballs, what if you could thrive because of them, transforming trials into catalysts for growth?

That's exactly what this chapter will help you uncover—the art of mental toughness. And I'm not talking about suppressing emotions or pretending to be invincible. No, this is about building real resilience on multiple levels—your mindset, behavior, and emotional landscape. With this skill, you don't just withstand turbulence; you harness it to elevate your life's trajectory.

Over the course of this chapter, you'll come to intimately understand what mental toughness is, why it matters, and how to cultivate this extraordinary aptitude accessible to us all. Consider this your invitation to stop avoiding adversity and start befriending it on your own terms. Life's obstacles need not break you; they can propel your evolution if you let them. That's the secret this chapter whispers.

We begin our journey by clearly defining mental toughness—what it is and what it is not. With insightful examples and vital background context, you quickly grasp this nebulous concept and all its subtleties. Then, we explore the invaluable role resilience plays in anchoring one's mental strength, especially during storms. You uncover why resilience and toughness are two threads of the same cloth.

As we delve deeper, you gain clarity on common barricades that inhibit mental toughness—from stress and peer pressure to emotional repression. By understanding these obstacles, you're empowered to circumvent them through mindset shifts and coping outlets illuminated later on. Knowledge of barriers is just as crucial as mapping the destination.

This chapter also addresses a pivotal question: What is the linkage between mental health disorders like anxiety, depression, OCD, and trauma and one's capacity for mental fortitude when hardship strikes? You gain insight into the skillful management of psychological issues to reinforce grit even on difficult days.

By the close of this information-packed chapter, your mental schema around adversity will transform radically. No longer an unwelcome interruption, adversity becomes a grooming tool forging you into the mentally toughest, most emotionally flexible version of yourself. Equipped with this multidimensional understanding of mental toughness, you ultimately shift from crisis victim to crisis alchemist.

What Is Mental Toughness?

Mental toughness refers to the ability to withstand or cope with challenges and bounce back from adversity. It involves being resilient on an emotional level to stress, obstacles, and difficult situations without falling apart. Individuals with high mental toughness are able to adapt to changing dynamics, overcome doubts within themselves, and persist through hardships to achieve their goals.

Mental toughness is often contrasted with mental weakness, which entails crumbling under pressure, being unable to manage emotions, dwelling on failures, and giving up easily when faced with roadblocks or criticism. Those lacking mental toughness become frequently overwhelmed by stress, make excuses, or fold at the first sign of conflict.

On the other hand, the mentally tough approach hardships with flexibility, emotional stability, and an internal locus of control. This enables them to navigate turbulence without losing composure or hope. While mental toughness does not make someone immune to discomfort or pain, it provides the grit and resilience to confront challenges constructively.

Understanding Resilience

Resilience is closely tied to mental toughness and can be described as the ability to positively adapt to and bounce back from adversity. It's that deep-rooted, steadfast spirit that helps individuals not only power through obstacles but grow because of them.

Resilience works hand-in-hand with mental toughness to provide the emotional, mental, and behavioral flexibility needed to tackle difficulties. Resilient people are able to acknowledge hard truths, take decisive action, and withstand the discomfort that often accompanies tribulations. Additionally, they are willing to ask for help when needed while accepting what is out of their control.

Essentially, resilience is the conduit that converts mentally tough attitudes into mentally tough actions. With resilience, one can anchor themselves emotionally during storms and fluidly navigate to calmer waters. Both resilience and mental toughness are lifelong skills developed through self-management, intentional practice, and learned optimism. Together, they produce the grit we need to thrive.

The Benefits of Resilience

Resilience is one of the most valuable tools we can cultivate to lead satisfying and meaningful lives. It allows us to not only endure trials but extract wisdom from them. By leveraging resilience, we turn life's stumbling blocks into stepping stones toward growth. Let's explore some of the key benefits this crucial skill offers:

Enhanced Mental Health

Resilience enables us to safeguard our emotional well-being when faced with potential triggers like grief, job loss, discrimination, or trauma. Resilient thinking patterns act as a shield, helping us view challenges through a lens of hope and possibility. This protects us from descending into states of anxiety, depression, or chronic stress when difficulties arise.

Strengthened Relationships

Coping with adversity requires patience, understanding, and perspective—all qualities nurtured by resilience. By developing resilience, we become better equipped to resolve interpersonal conflicts, offer support during tough times, and celebrate loved ones' wins. This creates an environment where relationships can deepen despite life's inevitable ups and downs.

Increased Self-Efficacy

Resilience boosts our ability to bounce back from failures and disappointments. By learning to reframe setbacks as opportunities for growth, we nurture our self-confidence to pick ourselves up, try again, and pursue our goals relentlessly. This motivates us to live courageously and overcome fears holding us back.

Enhanced Problem-Solving Abilities

Looking adversity squarely in the eyes requires critical thinking, resourcefulness, and level-headedness. Resilience strengthens these qualities, empowering us to analyze challenges, devise solutions, and execute them with flexibility. We move from reactive to responsive, getting ahead of obstacles with strategic action.

Expanded Coping Abilities

Resilience allows us to boost our tolerance for discomfort, uncertainty, and imperfection. By leaning into difficult emotions rather than avoiding them, we increase our distress tolerance skills over time. We realize we can experience painful feelings without being defined or debilitated by them.

In essence, resilience is the secret weapon that enables us to thrive amidst adversity. It allows us to tap into previously unknown reserves of internal strength and wisdom during life's most difficult chapters. Resilience is what separates surviving from truly living.

Barriers to Being Tough

While mental toughness offers profound benefits, cultivating it requires first recognizing and overcoming common barriers that erode emotional resilience. Two of the most significant obstacles are rumination and unhealthy stress levels.

Rumination and Stress

Rumination refers to the tendency to repetitively dwell on the causes, meanings, and consequences of one's negative emotions, problems, and life situations. It involves persistent and recurring thoughts that become excessive, intrusive, and distressing over time.

When an individual experiences a setback or difficult scenario, ruminating as an initial coping mechanism can be healthy to make sense of challenges. However, continually rehashing negatives beyond that point can fuel anxiety and maintain depressive moods.

Rumination essentially entraps people in a vicious thought cycle that exacerbates and prolongs psychological pain rather than leading to constructive solutions. In the long term, this erosion of emotional equilibrium hampers mental toughness significantly.

Additionally, unchecked stress often goes hand-in-hand with rumination, especially related to work, finances, relationships, trauma, or health issues. While occasional bouts of stress are unavoidable, chronic high stress magnifies emotional turbulence.

Without positive coping outlets, people rely even more heavily on rumination to manage elevated stress and negative emotions. This forms an unhealthy reinforcing loop where stress encourages rumination and rumination intensifies stress. Over time, individuals burn through their resilience reserves faster during crises, making constructive responses challenging.

Rumination and excessive stress are two linked pitfalls that can profoundly deplete our mental toughness, emotional flexibility, and psychological stamina over time if left unmanaged. Learning to reroute rumination while proactively addressing stress is pivotal for resilience.

People Pleasing and Peer Pressure

Many of us have a natural tendency to want approval from others. However, taken to an extreme, people-pleasing tendencies can undermine resilience and mental toughness. When our sense of self-worth rests predominantly on external validation, we become emotionally fragile.

People-pleasers often overextend themselves, trying to meet everyone's expectations. This leads to suppressed inner needs, poor boundaries, and diminished self-care. Unable to say no, they take on increasing burdens until daily life feels chronically overwhelming. This erosion of personal power leaves minimal inner reserves to tackle bigger adversities.

Additionally, the failure to stand firm often draws increasing disrespect from others over time. People-pleasers' inability to voice their true needs trains manipulators how little it takes to coerce them into uncomfortable situations. This further aggravates stress, anxiety, resentment, and despair.

Peer pressure produces similar outcomes. When people-pleasers constantly conform to their peers' desires rather than honoring their own, it breeds inauthenticity and self-betrayal. Not only do they attract peers who pressure them into riskier behaviors, but they also lose touch with their inner compass. This makes it exponentially harder to demonstrate resilience during crises.

In short, people-pleasing and peer pressure tend to lock us into an endless tailspin of external validation-seeking and inner insecurity. This quicksand must be avoided at all costs to develop lasting mental toughness. We must learn to stand confidently in ourselves and walk our own path, no matter how lonely it may be at times. With inner surety comes outer resilience.

Being Cold vs. Being Tough

In striving to become more mentally tough, it's easy to confuse this with being emotionally cold, detached, or unfeeling. However, the two could not be more different. Genuine mental toughness does not require ignoring your emotions; in fact, it relies on embracing the full spectrum of emotions with agility.

Being cold typically involves shutting out or numbing difficult feelings like grief, heartbreak, fear, or vulnerability. People who resort to emotional coldness often do so due to past traumas or attachment issues that left them wary of revealing sensitivity. By keeping others at bay and sealing off their inner world, they shield themselves from recurring hurts.

However, this emotional barricading exacts steep costs: isolation, loneliness, and inability to form intimate bonds. It also tends to fail during life's hardest blows, when suppressed emotions inevitably erupt like pressure cookers. In short, emotional coldness provides the illusion of strength while masking extreme brittleness.

In contrast, mentally tough individuals understand emotions and provide data worth examining, not weaknesses needing eradication. Instead of repressing vulnerability, the emotionally agile leverages it to build deeper connections, gain wisdom, and ask for needed support during rough patches. Rather than disconnecting from their feelings, the mentally tough nurture their entire inner ecosystem for optimum functioning during storms.

While being cold may mistakenly seem like a quick fix for those afraid of emotional overwhelm, it inhibits authentic relationships and lasting resilience. Conversely, mental toughness acknowledges strength and vulnerability are two sides of the same beautiful coin —both essential for living fully and compassionately no matter what comes.

Mental Health

Our mental health status exerts an enormous influence on our capacity for resilience and mental fortitude. When disorders like chronic anxiety, clinical depression, or post-traumatic stress intrude, they chip away at the bedrock supporting the emotional endurance needed to withstand crises.

Anxiety

Anxiety disorders foster prolonged emotional distress, irrational fears, excessive rumination, and avoidant behaviors—all impediments to strength during turbulence. Additionally, research indicates chronic anxiety correlates to reduced resilience after traumatic events due to diminished self-efficacy and learned helplessness (Charney, 2003).

Those suffering from anxiety often struggle to utilize positive reappraisals when faced with situations triggering unease and panic. This inhibits access to inner reserves that facilitate coping. Essentially, anxiety narrows our ability to process challenges logically and demonstrate mental agility.

Depression

Depression's gloomy influence on thought patterns and energy levels can profoundly diminish mental toughness. Those enduring major depressive episodes frequently find past resilience strategies ineffective, as the disorder often severs links between past wins and current self-efficacy.

Additionally, depression is characterized by amplified self-criticism, hopelessness about the future, and isolation from social support—all immunity dampeners when trials strike. By impairing executive function and cognitive flexibility, depression makes summoning our grit exponentially harder.

Other Conditions

Research shows a myriad of other diagnoses, like obsessive-compulsive disorder (OCD), schizophrenia, and borderline personality disorder, often coincide with depleted resilience markers in the wake of adversity (Porter et al., 2019). Additionally, compounding life stressors like divorce, the deaths of loved ones, or economic instability frequently correspond to accelerated erosion of individuals' mental and emotional stamina.

While mental toughness can certainly coexist with mental health issues given appropriate treatment, poor psychological health undoubtedly weakens individuals' baseline ability to withstand and recover from crises. Seeking help through counseling, medication, mindfulness practices, exercise, social connection, and healthy outlets can reinforce reserves.

Wrapping Up...

In this chapter, we've laid the groundwork for deeply comprehending mental toughness—what it entails, why it matters, and how to cultivate it. We've seen that genuine mental strength relies not on emotional repression but on resilience, adaptability, and wisdom in the face of challenges.

We've covered key concepts including

- the principles of mental toughness and its role in resilience
- common obstacles like stress, rumination, and peer pressure
- the impact of mental health on fortifying inner grit
- transforming life's curveballs from crises into catalysts

Understanding mental toughness is setting the foundation for living life undaunted by external turbulence. By recognizing adversity as a school rather than a threat, we open ourselves to profound learning and self-actualization. Equipped with this knowledge, we're now ready to embark upon the seven-step training program for developing unassailable mental strength.

In the next chapter, we begin this journey by tackling the epidemic of overthinking and freeing ourselves from its confines. You'll discover targeted techniques from mindfulness to mental pattern rewiring to gain supremacy over your inner world. Understanding mental toughness provides the vision; cultivating it is where the real work begins.

Case Study: Kate

When Kate lost her high-paying job of over a decade, her world turned upside down. As a single mom, she had depended on that job to provide a comfortable life for her two kids. Now, with her main source of income gone and few prospects on the horizon, she felt utterly overwhelmed and powerless.

Bills were piling up, her kids were stressed, and Kate's own mental health was deteriorating rapidly. She second-guessed all her career choices, wondering if she should have played it safer. Constant anxiety and sleepless nights left her exhausted and despairing. She began to isolate herself, withdrawing from friends and family out of shame.

In this storm of adversity, Kate desperately wished she could be mentally tougher—more resilient, more composed, more hopeful. But the sheer weight of her situation felt like a tidal wave knocking the wind out of her over and over again. She doubted she had the grit to come out of this catastrophe in one piece.

That's when Kate came across a book that talked about genuine mental strength coming not from faking positivity but from acknowledging difficult emotions. It didn't advise her to pretend she wasn't anxious or in financial trouble; it asked her to embrace the full gamut of emotions that accompany hardship. The book spoke to Kate's intuition that mental toughness wasn't about repressing fears or being invincible; it was about building resilience by moving through pain compassionately yet decisively.

Armed with this new perspective, Kate allowed herself to feel the ache of loss when staring at her empty bank account. But she also reminded herself that this intense anxiety would pass and better days awaited. She let tears flow after receiving yet another foreclosure warning but quickly refocused on compiling her resume. She felt the familiar pang of seeing ex-colleagues on social media but consciously shifted her attention to networking events.

The book also cautioned Kate about barriers that could erode mental toughness. Recognizing unhealthy rumination as an obstacle, she turned down the volume on relentless worrying by practicing mindfulness exercises. Scheduling regular meet-ups with supportive friends reinforced her coping mechanisms. Journaling helped her vent emotions and then strategize goals. Kate even tackled an anxiety disorder diagnosis proactively, unwilling to let it undermine her resilience.

Within a few months, Kate was interviewing for new positions with renewed confidence. By allowing herself to fully experience hardship without being debilitated, she emerged wiser and tougher. She landed a job that brought financial stability and even more fulfillment. Kate realized she didn't just want to survive adversity; she wanted to become its master.

Reflecting on her arduous journey, Kate saw everything she gained by walking through the fire—a deeper trust in her own abilities, indispensable coping tools, and profoundly empathetic relationships. She knew that the next life challenge might bring anxiety, but it would no longer bring despair. Kate had found an inner compass that now steered her not around but through troubles with scalpel-sharp awareness and unsinkable poise.

TWO

Step #1–Stop Overthinking in its Tracks

 *Do not judge me by my success; judge me by how many
times I fell down and got back up again.*

Nelson Mandela

Nelson Mandela's quote is the perfect mantra as we tackle
the common habit of overthinking that keeps tripping us
up mentally. In this chapter, we'll explore tools to break this cycle
of obsessive worrying so we can get back on our feet stronger than
before.

Together, we'll uncover easy yet effective ways to control our
runaway thoughts and focus our minds. First, we'll better understand why our brains get hooked on overanalyzing everything and
how this drains our mental and emotional energy. You'll learn
simple mindfulness practices to catch your thoughts before they
spiral and consciously shift your attention to calmer spaces.
Additionally, you'll acquire thought-challenging skills to dismantle

exaggerated, anxious thinking patterns and rewrite more balanced thought narratives.

As we go, supplementary coping ideas will come to light, including using healthy distractions to disrupt obsessive thoughts. You'll grasp why staying active and productive fights worry. And you'll discover how social bonds can ease anxiety. By the chapter's end, you'll have all the tools to kick overthinking to the curb for good and direct your thoughts toward your true priorities.

So let's start this empowering journey inspired by Mandela's wisdom not to judge ourselves by how often we stumble but by how often we rise back up.

Overthinking 101

If your mind often feels like a broken record, endlessly replaying worries on an anxious loop, you're no stranger to overthinking. But what exactly is this experience we call "overthinking," and how is it sabotaging our mental health? Let's explore its meaning, risks, and origins.

What Is Overthinking?

In short, overthinking refers to excessive, repetitive thoughts focused on negative outcomes, errors, or imperfections. It goes beyond productive problem-solving into unconstructive what-ifs and worst-case scenarios. Our analytical abilities shift from ally to adversary, conjuring exaggerated dangers rather than rational solutions.

Unlike fleeting bouts of everyday worrying, overthinking forms thought spirals that hijack attention for lengthy periods. These mental back-and-forths feed off uncertainty, transitions, perceived threats to ego, and changes beyond one's control—anything that disrupts normalcy. Overthinking entangles people in futile attempts to anticipate, prevent, or mentally resolve non-existent crises. This anguished mental wrestling yields little besides escalating anxiety and despair.

Overthinking vs. Rumination

Overthinking and rumination overlap significantly but have subtle distinctions. Rumination tends to fixate on negative personal traits, past failures, current problems without clear solutions, and bleak future scenarios. It carries a self-judgmental tone of blame and self-criticism.

In contrast, overthinking obsesses primarily over ambiguous external situations with possibly catastrophic implications. The spotlight centers on threat avoidance/mitigation rather than self-reproach. While rumination erodes self-worth, overthinking slowly poisons peace of mind. Both leave mental carnage in their wake.

Dangers of Overthinking

Overthinking unleashes a cascade of destructive consequences that wreak havoc on well-being. Fixating on emotionally charged "what-ifs" triggers chemical changes in the brain, raising stress hormones like cortisol. This heightens bodily sensations of anxiety —racing heart, tense muscles, insomnia. Not only does overthinking create distress in the moment, but chronic activation of the brain's fear pathways can fundamentally alter its structure and chemistry over time.

Additionally, overthinking often precipitates avoidance of potential emotional triggers or stressful situations. This shrinking social landscape breeds isolation and disconnection. As mood plummets, many fall into clinical anxiety or depression, needing professional treatment. In short, overthinking isn't just mentally exhausting; it's physiologically and emotionally corrosive.

Where Overthinking Comes From

Overthinking does not arise from innate character flaws or weaknesses. In fact, tendencies take root due to three primary causes: childhood conditioning, trauma response, or unsupportive environments. Growing up in chaotic, critical, or emotionally neglectful homes often wires overthinking patterns at a young age. Trauma also commonly triggers hypervigilant thoughts around safety and violation of trust. Additionally, cultural messaging plays a role, along with enabling relationships that reinforce obsessive worry. The seeds of overthinking scatter widely, but self-awareness and care can circumvent their sprouting.

Solution #1: Mindfulness

If your thoughts often feel like a broken record, playing the same worries on a loop, mindfulness can help you press stop. This first powerful solution helps you break free from exhausting mental loops and find inner peace.

What Is Mindfulness?

Mindfulness means focusing your awareness on the present moment. Instead of getting tangled up in regrets about the past or worries about the future, you purposefully redirect your focus to the here and now.

Mindfulness meditation strengthens this ability to stay grounded in the present. As thoughts come and go, you simply acknowledge them without judging them as good or bad. You don't latch onto them or get sucked into mental tunnels. You just gently shift your attention back to the now. This practice builds the mental muscle memory to catch yourself overthinking and hit pause.

How Mindfulness Helps Overthinking

Mindfulness helps in a few key ways. First, it builds awareness of when your mind wanders, preventing you from falling into obsessive thought trains. Noticing unhelpful thoughts early helps stop them from gaining momentum.

Second, mindfulness calms the brain's fear response centers which leads to stressful rumination. This reduces anxiety and boosts clear thinking.

Third, mindfulness reveals thoughts as passing events rather than absolute truths. This reduces extreme reactions to imagined worst-case scenarios.

Overall, by continually bringing your attention back to the present, mindfulness loosens overthinking's tight grip.

Daily Mindfulness Practices

We've explored how mindfulness helps minimize overthinking by grounding us in the present moment. But how do we actually integrate this state of mindful awareness into daily life? Establishing a regular mindfulness practice is key, and it can look different for everyone. The following exercises can take just a few minutes a day or longer, depending on your preferences and schedule. Just a few minutes a day can make a profound difference over time.

Here are some easy ways to build mindfulness and reduce over-thinking:

- Tune into your breathing—feel your belly rise and fall with each breath.
- Do a body scan—slowly scan your body from head to toe, noticing sensations.
- Take mindful nature walks—focus your senses on sights, sounds, and smells.
- Repeat a mantra—like "I am here now."
- Observe your thoughts as they arise and pass through your mind. Notice them without judgment or attachment, and imagine them floating by like clouds in the sky. As you witness the thoughts coming and going, you'll begin to recognize that you are not your thoughts, only the observer of your thoughts. This realization can help create a sense of detachment and perspective, allowing you to let go of rumination and overthinking more easily.

The key is not to latch onto thoughts but just let them drift on by. This mindful detachment from worries and obsession about the future is powerful. Give it a try!

Solution #2: Thought Challenging

If repetitive worrying has your mind spinning, thought challenging can help you regain control. By identifying and disputing distorted thought patterns driving your worries, this strategy helps shrink unhelpful thoughts down to size.

What Is Thought Challenging?

Thought challenging involves spotting worried thoughts that fuel anxiety, analyzing if they're accurate, and replacing them with balanced perspectives. Often called "distorted thoughts," these tend to amplify apprehension and tension.

Thought challenging starts by pinpointing distorted thoughts. Then, you reframe them to align better with reality. For example, instead of thinking, *I'll definitely mess up this presentation and be humiliated*, you might reframe it as, "I've gotten nervous before presentations but ended up doing fine. If I mess up a bit, it's not catastrophic." The goal is to develop fairer perspectives that keep you grounded.

Common Distorted Thought Patterns

Our minds often play tricks on us, skewing situations negatively. These exaggerated thought patterns are called "cognitive distortions"—and recognizing them helps us challenge anxious, worried thinking. Catching distortions quickly prevents them from fueling storms of overthinking.

To start restructuring imbalanced thinking, it helps to recognize common distorted thought patterns first, like:

- black-or-white thinking—only seeing extreme outcomes with no middle ground
- catastrophizing—assuming the worst-case scenario will for sure happen
- overgeneralization—believing one negative experience reflects an overall pattern
- emotional reasoning—basing conclusions only on feelings rather than facts

Catching and reframing distorted thoughts helps halt them in their tracks.

How to Challenge Thoughts

Once we identify our own characteristic distorted thoughts fueling overthinking, we can start challenging them. This simply means questioning their validity, finding more balanced perspectives, and ultimately quieting our worried inner voice.

To put thought challenging into action:

1. Identify worried, anxious thoughts and the distortions they demonstrate
2. Gather factual evidence against the distortions
3. Develop balanced responses aligned with reality
4. Repeat these new thoughts until they stick

For example, the thought *My friends didn't invite me out; they must not like me* shows emotional reasoning and overgeneralization. We would find evidence that this isn't totally true, like times when they included us. Our balanced response might be *Sometimes friends don't include me but often still want to spend time together.*

With practice, thought challenging retrains the brain's pathways away from exaggeration and toward clarity. Peace of mind can follow!

Solution #3: Distractions, Productivity, and Socializing

When overthinking gets intense, it often helps to shift your focus. Healthy distractions, staying productive, and social connections can help divert your mind from going in worried circles. Let's explore easy tips in each area:

Healthy Distractions

We all need a mental break sometimes from anxious thoughts spiraling out of control. Healthy distractions can provide that mental space and relief. By fully immersing our senses in an enjoyable activity, we halt the momentum of worries, letting them naturally fade into the background. Even a short distraction can help hit the reset button so we return with a clearer perspective.

It's fine to distract your mind briefly from distressing thoughts through

- reading an engrossing novel
- doing a puzzle or playing a game
- watching light-hearted shows
- listening to upbeat music
- going for a run or baking treats

Aim for distractions that fully capture your attention and lift your mood. This mental break can reboot your mind, letting worried thoughts naturally fade.

Staying Productive

Overthinking loves to flood in and occupy any mental space left unattended. An effective solution? Staying actively productive. By immersing yourself in constructive tasks and goals, you prevent unhelpful thoughts from monopolizing your mind. Achieving even small wins reinforces a sense of control and confidence to handle worries that eventually resurface with greater clarity.

Keep your momentum going by

- making to-do lists
- breaking big tasks into small steps
- rewarding progress to stay motivated
- scheduling activities to fill the time

Focusing your mental energy on productive tasks prevents over-thinking from filling the space. Achieving goals boosts confidence to tackle worries that resurface later with clarity.

Increase Your Socialization

Humans are social creatures at our core. During times of emotional turmoil like unrelenting overthinking, the support of caring connections can make all the difference. By voicing your inner worries to close friends and family, their encouragement and reassurance help diminish anxious thoughts' power over time. Even just spending an enjoyable time interacting with loved ones redirects your attention in a positive way.

Plan social activities like

- video chats to catch up with friends
- sharing coffee or meals together
- exercising alongside others
- attending social events virtually or locally

Meaningful connection is healing. Voice concerns openly to loved ones offering non-judgmental ears. Their support helps put anxious thoughts in perspective so they lose intensity over time.

The key is recognizing when overthinking starts hijacking your mind. Once you notice worried thoughts spinning, try shifting gears to any distraction, task, or person that can halt the mental loop and restore balance.

Exercise: Overthinking Trap

The goal of this written exercise is to help identify common over-thinking thought patterns you experience along with the situational triggers that tend to set them in motion. Bringing awareness to these thought traps is the first step in dismantling overthinking tendencies long term.

Let's get started:

Reflect on the last 2–3 times you notice yourself falling into obsessive, worrying thought spirals. These could be at night while trying to fall asleep, during work on challenging projects, in your relationships after disagreements, and so on. Any situation that hooks your mind into a whirling mental tunnel about possible negative outcomes.

Next, for each identified overthinking experience, document the following on a piece of paper, your phone, or a journal:

- What was the situation or trigger preceding the beginning of the thought spiral?
- What specific thoughts or fearful predictions did the overthinking episode revolve around?
- Were there themes or common distortions—like catastrophizing or black-or-white thinking—you tended to indulge around this topic?
- How much time did you spend overanalyzing before catching and redirecting yourself?
- On a 1–10 scale, how disruptive was this bout of overthinking to your productivity and inner peace?

Lastly, based on your observations from these documented over-thinking traps, summarize

- the most common triggers sending you into overthinking
- the top 3–5 thought distortion patterns you default to (ex. blowing things out proportion, imagining only worst-case outcomes, etc.)
- initial ideas for how to catch and combat overthinking when these known triggers and distortions are next activated

Use these revelations of your characteristic thought traps to fuel your motivation and strategy for short-circuiting overthinking going forward! Recognizing our own repeated sticky mental web patterns is illuminating for ultimately changing their trajectory toward wisdom and emotional freedom.

Wrapping Up...

In this first step forward, we've gained skills to stop obsessive worrying and take control of runaway thoughts. We're no longer trapped in tiring mental loops. Now, we can catch anxious thoughts before they spiral and intentionally shift our focus to clarity instead.

We've covered easy yet powerful techniques, including:

- mindfulness practices to ground us in the present
- thought challenging to dispute exaggerated, worried thinking
- helpful coping ideas like healthy distractions and social support

Learning to hit the brakes on a spinning mind paves the way to building real mental strength. By developing internal resilience first, we're better equipped to handle external storms down the road.

Now that we've conquered overthinking's maze, we'll learn how to master stress next. In the next chapter, we'll unlock secrets to responding skillfully to daily pressures and safeguarding our peace of mind. Armed with coping strategies, we'll keep strengthening our mental muscles for any challenge.

Case Study: Amara

Amara's mind had always tended to spiral into imagining worst-case scenarios ever since she was little. As a kid, her anxious thoughts often focused on family members being hurt or her life feeling unstable from moving a lot. As an adult, she channeled this overthinking tendency into excelling at her finance job, planning for every possible bad outcome in her projects.

At first, Amara's constant worrying brought promotions at work for her thorough planning. But over time, the strain of constant overthinking started impacting her health. She developed insomnia, migraines, and an ulcer by age 30. She desperately wished for mental strength to turn off her spinning thoughts when needed.

By chance, one sleepless night, Amara found a book on building mental toughness. She eagerly turned to the chapter called "Stop Overthinking in Its Tracks," hoping to understand and gain control over her exhausting thought spirals.

The chapter explained how brains prone to anxiety get wired to scan for threats on overdrive. Amara learned simple mindfulness practices to catch herself when worries accelerated and purpose-fully shifted her focus back to the present moment instead. Using a mantra like "I'm here now" helped ground her when anxious thoughts popped up.

Amara also began journaling to get the thoughts out of her head. This, along with techniques to challenge her exaggerated, worst-case obsessions, started retraining her brain toward balance. She posted reminders everywhere saying, "Am I overdoing this?" to trigger herself to rationally reassess scenarios sending her mind spinning.

With practice, Amara caught her mind wandering into anxious mental tunnels much sooner. Hours previously lost in obsessive analysis got redirected into constructive tasks and hobbies that boosted her confidence. Coffee dates and yoga classes with supportive friends eased residual anxiety. For the first time in decades, glimpses of calm appeared, like still waters after an endless storm. From that peace, authentic mental strength grew roots inside Amara.

Amara's overthinking tendencies still arise, but she now has tools to recognize and redirect them effectively. Her story offers hope to anyone locked in exhausting mental loops—we all can retrain our minds toward clarity and tranquility with dedication. By stopping overthinking in its tracks, we reset our path toward inner freedom.

THREE

Step #2—Managing Stress the Right Way

---

66 *If you can't fly, then run; if you can't run, then walk; if you can't walk, then crawl, but whatever you do, you have to keep moving forward.*

Martin Luther King Jr.

D r. King's words ring true when it comes to building mental strength and resilience. His quote is a powerful reminder that no matter how tough things get, we have to keep pushing forward, even if it means crawling at times. It's a message that applies to all of us as we navigate the ups and downs of life.

In the last chapter, we took the first step in our journey toward unshakable mental toughness by learning how to quiet the noise of overthinking. It's a skill that takes practice but one that can make a world of difference in our ability to stay focused and grounded in the face of challenges.

Now, we're turning our attention to another major roadblock on the path to mental toughness: stress. Let's face it—stress is a part of life. It's not something we can avoid altogether, but when we let it run rampant, it can take a serious toll on our mental and emotional well-being. It can leave us feeling drained, overwhelmed, and ill-equipped to handle the curve balls that life inevitably throws our way.

But here's the good news: By understanding how stress works and developing a toolbox of strategies to manage it effectively, we can minimize its negative impact and even harness it as a force for growth and resilience.

In this chapter, we're going to take a deep dive into the psychology of stress. We'll explore why we feel it in the first place, how it affects us both mentally and physically, and how we can tell the difference between stress that motivates us to step up our game and stress that tears us down.

But we won't stop at just understanding stress—you'll learn a range of powerful techniques for overcoming it. From simple lifestyle tweaks to relaxation practices to the transformative power of engaging in activities that light you up, you'll come away with a wealth of strategies for building stress resilience and mental toughness.

By the time you finish this chapter, you'll have the knowledge and tools you need to navigate life's challenges with poise, grace, and unwavering mental strength. So, let's dive in and start mastering the art of stress management—your journey to unshakable resilience starts now.

The Problem With Stress

Stress is an unavoidable part of life, affecting people from all walks of life and all age groups. It is a natural response to challenging or threatening situations, triggering a complex cascade of physiological and psychological reactions. While some stress can be beneficial, motivating us to take action and perform at our best, excessive or prolonged stress can have detrimental effects on our mental and physical well-being.

Why We Feel Stress: Psychological Understandings

From a psychological standpoint, stress arises when we perceive a situation as challenging, threatening, or beyond our ability to cope. Common stressors include work deadlines, financial pressures, relationship conflicts, health concerns, and major life changes. Our mind interprets these situations as potential threats to our well-being, triggering the body's stress response.

The stress response is orchestrated by the autonomic nervous system, which activates the "fight-or-flight" response. This ancient survival mechanism prepares the body to face or flee from danger by releasing stress hormones like cortisol and adrenaline. These hormones increase heart rate, blood pressure, and blood sugar levels while diverting energy away from non-essential functions like digestion and immune response.

In the short term, this stress response can enhance focus, alertness, and performance, helping us rise to the challenge at hand. This is often referred to as "good stress" or "eustress." However, when stress becomes chronic or overwhelming, it can take a toll on our mental and physical health. Prolonged exposure to stress hormones can lead to anxiety, depression, impaired cognitive function, weakened immune response, and increased risk of chronic diseases like heart disease and diabetes.

Moreover, our psychological response to stress is shaped by our thoughts, beliefs, and coping strategies. Negative self-talk, catastrophic thinking, and a lack of perceived control can amplify the impact of stress, leading to feelings of helplessness and despair. On the other hand, a positive mindset, effective problem-solving skills, and a strong support system can help buffer the effects of stress and promote resilience.

Understanding the psychological mechanisms of stress is crucial for developing effective stress management strategies. By recognizing the difference between good and bad stress and cultivating a healthy mindset and coping skills, we can harness the benefits of stress while minimizing its negative impact on our well-being.

Common Stressors

In today's fast-paced world, stress can stem from a wide range of sources. Some of the most common stressors include:

- **Work-related stress:** Job demands, long hours, tight deadlines, high-pressure environments, job insecurity, and conflicts with coworkers or supervisors can all contribute to work-related stress.
- **Financial stress:** Money worries, such as debt, bills, unexpected expenses, and financial instability, are a significant source of stress for many people.
- **Relationship stress:** Conflicts with partners, family members, or friends, as well as the stress of caregiving responsibilities or the loss of a loved one, can take a heavy emotional toll.
- **Health-related stress:** Chronic illnesses, injuries, or health scares can be highly stressful, as can the pressure to maintain a healthy lifestyle in the face of busy schedules and competing demands.

- **Major life changes:** Significant life transitions, such as moving, getting married, having a baby, or changing careers, can be exciting but also stressful as they require adaptation and adjustment.
- **Environmental stress:** Factors like noise pollution, traffic, crowding, and climate change can contribute to stress, particularly for those living in urban areas.
- **Social and political stress:** Social pressures, discrimination, and political tensions can be a source of stress, particularly for marginalized or disadvantaged groups.
- **Technology-related stress:** The constant connectivity and information overload of the digital age can lead to "technostress," as well as the stress of managing online relationships and social media pressures.

While these stressors are common, it's important to recognize that stress is a highly individual experience. What may be stressful for one person may not be for another, depending on factors like personality, coping skills, and life circumstances. By identifying our own unique stressors and developing personalized stress management strategies, we can better navigate the challenges of modern life and maintain our well-being in the face of stress.

Good vs. Bad Stress

Not all stress is created equal. While we often think of stress as a negative force, some stress can actually be beneficial. Psychologists often distinguish between "good stress" (also known as "eustress") and "bad stress" (or "distress").

Good stress is the kind of stress that energizes and motivates us. It's the excitement we feel when taking on a new challenge, the adrenaline rush of a looming deadline, or the butterflies in our stomachs before a big presentation. This type of stress can enhance our focus, creativity, and performance, pushing us to grow and achieve our goals. Good stress is typically short-lived and within our coping abilities.

Examples of good stress include:

- starting a new job or taking on a challenging project
- preparing for a wedding or other significant life event
- engaging in physical exercise or competition
- stepping outside of your comfort zone to learn a new skill

In contrast, bad stress is the kind of stress that overwhelms us and exceeds our ability to cope. It's the feeling of being buried under a mountain of responsibilities, the anxiety of a toxic work environment, or the exhaustion of caring for a chronically ill loved one. Bad stress is often chronic, meaning it persists over an extended period, and can lead to a host of negative physical and mental health outcomes.

Examples of bad stress include:

- enduring an abusive relationship
- struggling with chronic financial insecurity
- dealing with the aftermath of a traumatic event

The key difference between good and bad stress lies in our perception and response. Good stress feels manageable and meaningful, while bad stress feels overwhelming and beyond our control. Moreover, what may be good stress for one person may be bad stress for another, depending on individual resilience and coping skills.

In order to harness the benefits of good stress while minimizing the impact of bad stress, it's essential to develop effective stress management techniques. This may include practices like exercise, time management, and seeking support when needed. By learning to distinguish between good and bad stress and responding accordingly, we can cultivate a healthy relationship with stress that allows us to thrive in the face of life's challenges.

Solution #1: Lifestyle Changes

Making simple lifestyle changes can have a profound impact on reducing stress and building mental toughness. By focusing on three key areas—diet, exercise, and sleep—you can create a solid foundation for managing stress effectively.

Diet

What you eat can significantly influence your stress levels and overall mental well-being. A healthy, balanced diet rich in whole foods, fruits, vegetables, lean proteins, and healthy fats can help regulate mood, improve energy levels, and support brain function.

When you're stressed, your body releases cortisol, a hormone that can trigger cravings for high-fat, high-sugar foods. While these foods may provide temporary comfort, they can ultimately lead to feelings of guilt, sluggishness, and increased stress. By making healthier food choices, you can help break this cycle and support your body's natural stress-fighting abilities.

To make better dietary choices for stress management:

- **Incorporate stress-reducing foods:** Certain foods, such as dark chocolate, nuts, seeds, fatty fish, and avocados, contain nutrients that can help reduce stress and promote relaxation. For example, dark chocolate is rich in magnesium, which can help regulate cortisol levels, while fatty fish like salmon and tuna are high in omega-3 fatty acids, which have been shown to reduce inflammation and support brain health.

- **Limit processed and sugary foods:** These foods can cause blood sugar spikes and crashes, leading to increased stress and anxiety. They also tend to be low in nutrients and high in empty calories, which can contribute to feelings of fatigue and irritability. Instead, opt for whole, unprocessed foods that provide sustained energy and essential vitamins and minerals.

- **Stay hydrated:** Dehydration can exacerbate feelings of stress and fatigue, so aim to drink plenty of water throughout the day. Even mild dehydration can lead to headaches, difficulty concentrating, and mood changes. Keep a water bottle with you and sip regularly, especially during stressful situations.

- **Practice mindful eating:** Take the time to sit down and enjoy your meals without distractions, paying attention to the flavors, textures, and sensations of your food. Mindful eating can help you tune in to your body's hunger and fullness cues, reducing the likelihood of stress-related overeating. It also allows you to savor and appreciate your food, turning mealtime into a relaxing and enjoyable experience.

- **Plan ahead:** Stress can often lead to impulsive food choices, so it's helpful to plan your meals and snacks in advance. Prepare healthy options like cut vegetables, hummus, or trail mix to have on hand when cravings strike. When you have a busy day ahead, pack a nutritious lunch and snacks to avoid relying on fast food or vending machines.

Exercise

Regular physical activity is one of the most effective ways to combat stress and build mental toughness. Exercise releases endorphins, the body's natural mood boosters, and helps reduce stress hormones like cortisol. It also improves sleep quality, boosts self-confidence, and provides a healthy outlet for frustration and anxiety.

When you exercise, your body undergoes physiological changes that help reduce stress and improve overall well-being. Your heart rate increases, your breathing deepens, and your muscles work harder, all of which can help release tension and improve circulation. Over time, regular exercise can also help you build resilience to stress, making it easier to cope with challenging situations.

To incorporate exercise into your stress management routine:

- **Find activities you enjoy:** Whether it's walking, swimming, dancing, or playing a sport, choose exercises that you find enjoyable and sustainable. When you look forward to your workouts, you're more likely to stick with them long-term. Experiment with different activities until you find ones that resonate with you.
- **Start small:** If you're new to exercise, begin with just a few minutes a day and gradually increase the duration and intensity over time. Even a short, 10-minute walk can provide stress-reducing benefits.
- **Make it a habit:** Consistency is key when it comes to reaping the stress-reducing benefits of exercise. Aim to

incorporate physical activity into your daily routine, even if it's just a short walk during your lunch break. Schedule your workouts like you would any other important appointment, and treat them as non-negotiable self-care time.

- **Try stress-specific exercises:** Certain activities, such as yoga, tai chi, and Qigong, are particularly effective for reducing stress and promoting relaxation. These practices combine physical movement with deep breathing and meditation, helping to calm the mind and release tension in the body. Consider attending a class or following along with a video to learn proper technique and form.
- **Get outside:** Exercising in nature can provide additional stress-reducing benefits. Exposure to greenery, fresh air, and natural light can help improve mood, reduce anxiety, and promote a sense of calm. Take a hike, go for a bike ride, or simply do your regular workout in a nearby park or beach.

Sleep

Getting enough quality sleep is essential for managing stress and maintaining mental toughness. Sleep deprivation can exacerbate feelings of stress, anxiety, and irritability while also impairing cognitive function and decision-making skills.

During sleep, your body undergoes important restorative processes, including the release of growth hormones, tissue repair, and memory consolidation. Lack of sleep can disrupt these processes, leading to increased inflammation, weakened immune function, and impaired emotional regulation. Over time, chronic sleep deprivation can take a serious toll on both physical and mental health.

Steps to improve your sleep so you can better manage stress include:

- **Establish a consistent sleep schedule:** Go to bed and wake up at the same time to establish a strong internal clock pattern. Consistency is key, as even small variations in sleep timing can disrupt your sleep quality.
- **Create a relaxing bedtime routine:** Develop a calming pre-sleep ritual, such as taking a warm bath, reading a book, or practicing relaxation techniques like deep breathing or meditation. Having rituals tells your body that it's time to start winding down. Avoid stimulating activities like watching TV or scrolling through social media, as these can make it harder to fall asleep.
- **Optimize your sleep environment:** Ensure your bedroom is cool, quiet, and dark, and invest in a comfortable mattress and pillows. Use earplugs or a white noise machine to block out disruptive sounds, and consider using blackout curtains or an eye mask to eliminate light pollution. Keep your bedroom tidy and clutter-free to promote a sense of calm and relaxation.
- **Limit screen time before bed:** The blue light emitted by electronic devices can interfere with your body's natural sleep-wake cycle, so try to avoid screens for at least an hour before bedtime. If you must use a device, consider using blue light-blocking glasses or installing a blue light filter app to reduce your exposure.
- **Avoid caffeine and alcohol close to bedtime:** These substances can disrupt sleep quality and make it harder to fall asleep. Caffeine can stay in your system for up to eight hours, so it's best to avoid it after lunchtime. While alcohol may initially make you feel drowsy, it can interfere with

deep, restorative sleep and cause middle-of-the-night awakenings.

- **Practice good sleep hygiene:** In addition to the above tips, there are several other habits that can promote better sleep. Avoid large meals, intense exercise, and stressful activities close to bedtime. Keep your bedroom temperature cool, around 60–67°F (15–19°C). If you can't fall asleep within 20–30 minutes, get out of bed and do a calming activity until you feel sleepy.

By making these lifestyle changes and prioritizing diet, exercise, and sleep, you can significantly reduce your stress levels, build mental toughness, and improve your overall well-being. Remember that change takes time, and it's okay to start small and gradually build upon your progress. Be patient with yourself, celebrate your successes, and don't hesitate to seek support from friends, family, or a mental health professional if needed.

Solution #2: Relaxation Techniques

Incorporating relaxation techniques, such as breathing exercises and meditation, into your daily routine can be a powerful way to manage stress and promote a sense of calm and well-being. These practices help activate the body's natural relaxation response, reducing stress hormones, lowering blood pressure, and promoting feelings of peace and tranquility.

Breathing

Breathing exercises are a simple yet effective way to reduce stress and anxiety. When you're stressed, your breathing tends to become shallow and rapid, which can exacerbate feelings of tension and unease. By consciously slowing down and deepening your breath, you can signal to your body that it's time to relax and unwind.

Here are three breathing techniques to try:

- **Diaphragmatic breathing:** The key here is to focus on breathing deeply into your diaphragm, rather than taking shallow breaths into your chest. To do this, place one hand on your chest and the other on your belly. As you inhale slowly through your nose, you should feel your belly rise like a balloon filling with air. Then, exhale slowly through pursed lips, as if you're blowing out a candle, and feel your belly fall. Aim for 5-10 breaths like this, and you'll be amazed at how much calmer you feel.
- **4-7-8 breathing:** Find a comfortable seated position with your back straight, and place the tip of your tongue against the ridge behind your upper front teeth. Start by exhaling completely through your mouth, making a "whoosh" sound. Then, close your mouth and quietly inhale through your nose for a count of 4. Hold that breath for a count of 7, and then exhale completely through your mouth (making that "whoosh" sound again) for a count of 8. Repeat this cycle 3–4 times, and feel your worries start to melt away.
- **Alternate nostril breathing:** This yogic technique is said to help balance the left and right hemispheres of the brain, promoting relaxation and mental clarity. To try it, sit comfortably with your back straight and rest your left hand on your lap. Use your right thumb to gently close your right nostril, and take a deep breath in through your left nostril. Then, close your left nostril with your ring finger, release your thumb from your right nostril, and exhale through your right nostril. Now, inhale through

your right nostril, close it with your thumb, release your ring finger from your left nostril, and exhale through your left nostril. Repeat this pattern for 5-10 cycles, and notice how much more centered and focused you feel.

Meditation

Meditation is a powerful tool for reducing stress, improving focus, and cultivating a sense of inner peace. By training your mind to be present and non-judgmental, you can learn to observe your thoughts and emotions without getting caught up in them, reducing their power to cause stress and anxiety.

Here are two guided meditations to try:

- **Body scan meditation:** This meditation involves systematically focusing on each part of your body, from your toes to your head, bringing awareness to any sensations or tension you may feel. Lie down or sit comfortably with your eyes closed. Take a few deep breaths, allowing your body to settle. Starting with your toes, bring your attention to any sensations you feel in that part of your body. If you notice any tension, imagine your breath flowing into that area, releasing and relaxing it. Slowly move your attention up your body, focusing on each part in turn until you reach the top of your head. Allow yourself to rest in a state of relaxed awareness for a few moments before gently opening your eyes.
- **Loving-kindness meditation:** This meditation involves cultivating feelings of love, compassion, and goodwill toward yourself and others. Sit comfortably with your eyes closed. Take a few deep breaths, allowing your body to settle. Bring to mind someone you love and appreciate,

and silently repeat the following phrases: "May you be happy. May you be healthy. May you be safe. May you live with ease." Next, bring to mind someone you feel neutral toward, and repeat the phrases. Then, bring to mind someone you find challenging, and repeat the phrases. Finally, extend these feelings of loving-kindness to all beings everywhere, silently repeating: "May all beings be happy. May all beings be healthy. May all beings be safe. May all beings live with ease."

Remember, the key to benefiting from relaxation techniques is consistency. Aim to practice your chosen techniques for at least 5–10 minutes a day, gradually increasing the duration as you become more comfortable. It may feel challenging at first, but with regular practice, you'll find it easier to quiet your mind and tap into a sense of inner calm.

In addition to breathing exercises and meditation, there are many other relaxation techniques to explore, such as progressive muscle relaxation, visualization, and yoga. Experiment with different techniques to find what works best for you, and don't hesitate to seek guidance from a qualified instructor or therapist if needed.

By incorporating relaxation techniques into your daily routine, you can cultivate a greater sense of resilience and equanimity in the face of life's challenges. These practices can help you stay grounded, focused, and calm, even in the midst of stress and uncertainty. With regular practice, you'll develop a powerful set of tools for managing stress, improving your well-being, and enhancing your overall quality of life.

Solution #3: Do What You Love

Engaging in hobbies and activities that bring you joy and fulfill-ment can be a powerful way to reduce stress, improve your mental well-being, and build mental toughness. When you immerse your-self in an activity you love, you create a sense of flow and mindful-ness that can help you forget about your worries and stressors, even if only for a little while.

How Hobbies Improve Stress Levels

Hobbies provide a much-needed break from the demands and pressures of daily life, allowing you to recharge your batteries and return to your responsibilities with renewed energy and focus. When you engage in an activity you enjoy, your body releases endorphins, the natural mood-boosting chemicals that promote feelings of happiness and well-being.

In addition to providing a sense of pleasure and accomplishment, hobbies can also help you develop new skills, build social connec-tions, and cultivate a sense of purpose and meaning. All of these factors can contribute to greater resilience and mental toughness in the face of stress and adversity.

Some of the ways hobbies can improve stress levels include:

- **Providing a sense of control:** When you engage in a hobby, you have the power to choose what you do and how you do it. This sense of control can be especially valuable during times of stress, when many aspects of life may feel outside of your control.
- **Promoting mindfulness:** Hobbies that require focus and concentration, such as painting, gardening, or playing an instrument, can help you cultivate a sense of mindfulness

and presence. By immersing yourself in the task at hand, you can quiet your mind and find relief from stress and worry.

- **Boosting self-esteem:** As you develop new skills and achieve goals related to your hobby, you'll likely experience a sense of pride and accomplishment. This can help boost your self-esteem and confidence, making you feel more capable of handling life's challenges.
- **Providing social support:** Many hobbies involve interacting with others who share your interests, whether through clubs, classes, or online communities. These social connections can provide a valuable source of support and camaraderie during times of stress.

Best Hobbies for Stress Relief

The best hobby for stress relief is one that you genuinely enjoy and look forward to. That said, certain types of hobbies may be particularly beneficial for reducing stress and promoting relaxation. Here are a few ideas:

- **Creative pursuits:** Engaging in creative activities, such as drawing, painting, writing, or crafting, can be a powerful way to express your emotions, process stress, and find a sense of calm and focus. These hobbies allow you to enter a state of flow, where you become fully absorbed in the task at hand and forget about your worries.
- **Physical activities:** Exercise is a well-known stress reliever, and hobbies that involve physical activity can be especially beneficial. Whether it's dancing, hiking, cycling, or playing a sport, moving your body can help release tension, boost your mood, and improve your overall sense of well-being.

- **Gardening and nature-based activities:** Spending time in nature has been shown to reduce stress, improve mood, and promote feelings of peace and tranquility. Hobbies such as gardening, birdwatching, or nature photography can help you connect with the natural world and find a sense of grounding and perspective.
- **Learning and intellectual pursuits:** Engaging in hobbies that challenge your mind, such as reading, learning a new language, or playing chess, can help you stay mentally sharp and engaged. These activities provide a sense of accomplishment and can help you maintain a positive outlook even during difficult times.

Remember, the key to using hobbies for stress relief is to choose activities that you genuinely enjoy and that fit your lifestyle and preferences. Don't be afraid to try new things and experiment until you find hobbies that resonate with you.

By making time for hobbies and activities that bring you joy and fulfillment, you can create a powerful buffer against stress and build greater mental toughness and resilience. These practices can help you stay grounded, focused, and positive, even in the face of life's challenges. So, whether it's picking up a paintbrush, lacing up your hiking boots, or rolling out your yoga mat, make sure to prioritize doing what you love as part of your overall stress management strategy.

Wrapping Up...

In this chapter, we took a deep dive into the world of stress management, exploring effective strategies for reducing stress and building mental toughness. By making simple lifestyle changes and incorporating relaxation techniques into your daily routine, you can significantly improve your ability to handle life's challenges with grace and resilience.

We've covered a range of powerful tools, including:

- optimizing your diet, exercise, and sleep habits to create a solid foundation for stress management
- practicing breathing exercises to activate your body's natural relaxation response and promote feelings of calm
- incorporating meditation into your daily routine to cultivate mindfulness, focus, and inner peace
- engaging in activities that you love and bring you joy

Learning to manage stress effectively is a crucial component of developing mental toughness. By taking proactive steps to reduce stress and promote well-being, you'll be better equipped to navigate life's ups and downs with clarity, resilience, and strength.

Now that we've mastered the art of stress management, we'll turn our attention to the power of emotional agility. In the next chapter, we'll explore how developing emotional agility can help you navigate complex feelings, accept and utilize emotions effectively, and further strengthen your mental toughness. Get ready to discover the transformative potential of cultivating emotional agility and nurturing your inner resilience.

Case Study: Michael

Meet Michael, a 40-year-old software engineer who thought he had it all figured out when it came to dealing with pressure. He was the guy who always stepped up when deadlines were tight, working long hours and subsisting on a diet of coffee and takeout. He wore his ability to handle stress like a badge of honor.

However, as the years went by and the demands on his time and energy kept piling up, Michael started to feel the cracks in his armor. He was snapping at coworkers, struggling to focus, and feeling like he was constantly running on empty. His once-active lifestyle had fallen by the wayside, replaced by late nights at the office and a growing sense of overwhelm.

It was a wake-up call for Michael when he realized that his "push through it" approach to stress management just wasn't cutting it anymore. He knew he needed to make some changes if he wanted to get his mental well-being back on track.

So, he started small. He began by taking a hard look at his diet and making some simple swaps—more nuts and seeds for snacks, less caffeine, and plenty of water to stay hydrated. He dusted off his old basketball and joined a local league, committing to weekly games as a way to get moving and blow off some steam. He started biking to work, using the morning ride as a chance to clear his head and set a positive tone for the day.

Next, Michael turned his attention to his sleep habits. He created a relaxing bedtime routine, complete with stretching and journaling and invested in a comfortable new mattress and pillows. He also started experimenting with relaxation techniques, like deep breathing and mindfulness meditation, to help calm his racing thoughts and ease feelings of anxiety.

As Michael started to prioritize his physical and mental health, he noticed a shift in his ability to handle stress. He was able to approach challenges at work with a clearer head and a more resilient mindset. His relationships with colleagues and loved ones improved as he learned to communicate more effectively and respond to pressure in a healthier way.

Through this journey, Michael discovered that building mental toughness isn't about burning the candle at both ends or pushing yourself to the brink of exhaustion. It's about developing a toolkit of strategies and habits that allow you to navigate life's inevitable stresses with grace and resilience.

By making simple changes to his lifestyle and incorporating relaxation techniques into his daily routine, Michael was able to transform his relationship with stress and cultivate the mental strength he needed to thrive—both at work and in his personal life.

His story is a powerful reminder that no matter how overwhelming stress may feel in the moment, we all have the power to take control of our well-being and build the mental toughness we need to overcome any obstacle that comes our way.

FOUR

Step #3—Honing Emotional Agility

> *Out of suffering have emerged the strongest souls; the most massive characters are seared with scars.*
>
> Khalil Gibran

Life is full of ups and downs, joys and sorrows, triumphs and challenges. No matter how mentally tough or resilient you are, you will inevitably encounter difficult emotions along the way —grief, fear, anger, shame, disappointment. The key to thriving in the face of adversity is not to avoid or suppress these feelings but to develop the agility to face them courageously and use them as fuel for growth.

This is where emotional agility comes in. Emotional agility is the ability to be with your emotions in a healthy way—to acknowledge and accept your inner experiences without being controlled by them. It's about treating your feelings as data to learn from rather than directives you must blindly obey. With emotional agility, you cultivate the flexibility and resilience to deal with life's challenges and changes with grace, clarity, and purposeful action.

In this chapter, you'll learn the mindsets and skills of emotional agility. You'll discover how to be aware of your emotions without being swept away by them, question your thoughts and assumptions, and choose intentional responses aligned with your values. No longer will you be at the mercy of knee-jerk reactions or emotional storms. Instead, you'll be able to navigate your inner world like a skilled captain at the helm of a ship—aware of the changing tides and weather but steering your course with wisdom and intention.

Emotional agility is a superpower that enables you to extract the lessons and growth opportunities from any adversity. When you can acknowledge the full depths of your emotional world with honesty and self-compassion, you liberate yourself from suffering and struggle. You gain access to your inner reserves of clarity, creativity and coping. Challenges become chances to evolve and emotions become allies on the path to meaning and mastery.

Get ready to radically transform your relationship with your emotions and upgrade your mental toughness with the skills of emotional agility. By the end of this chapter, you'll have potent tools and techniques to navigate the inevitable ups and downs of life with unwavering inner strength and flexibility. True freedom, fulfillment and resilience await as you learn to embrace the power of emotional agility.

What Is Emotional Agility?

Emotional agility is the ability to experience your thoughts, emotions, and events in a way that doesn't drive you in negative directions but instead encourages you to reveal the best of yourself. Rather than ignoring difficult emotions or getting swept away by them, emotional agility is about facing your inner experiences with courage and compassion and then choosing how to move forward intentionally in line with your values and goals.

Picture a tree in the midst of a storm, battered by heavy winds and rain. Its branches sway and bend with the gusts, but ultimately, the tree remains rooted and grounded. It adapts to the changing conditions without snapping or toppling over. This is what emotional agility looks like—having the flexibility, strength, and resilience to navigate life's ups and downs while staying true to yourself and what matters most to you.

When you cultivate emotional agility, you allow yourself to feel the full range of emotions, even the unpleasant ones, without getting hooked by them. You acknowledge and accept what you're feeling, understand where those feelings are coming from, and then proactively choose how to respond rather than reacting on autopilot. You maintain clarity about your deepest priorities so you can align your actions with your values, even when faced with stress or adversity.

With emotional agility, you learn to experience emotions as transient states that come and go, like clouds passing across the sky. Instead of identifying with your feelings or viewing them as permanent reflections of who you are, you recognize them as temporary experiences to learn from as you continue moving forward purposefully. Emotional agility empowers you to be courageous, vulnerable, and resilient as you navigate the inevitable complexities of life and work. It frees you up to engage fully, take risks, and thrive.

Benefits of Emotional Agility

Cultivating emotional agility provides a multitude of powerful benefits that can transform your life, work, and relationships for the better. When you develop the skills to mindfully navigate your inner world, you open the door to greater resilience, authenticity, and effectiveness.

One of the key advantages of emotional agility is improved psychological health and well-being. By learning to face and accept the full range of your emotions, you build distress tolerance and reduce emotional suffering. You're less likely to get trapped in toxic cycles of rumination, blame, or avoidance. This frees up mental and emotional bandwidth so you can focus on what truly matters.

Emotional agility also fosters stronger, more authentic relationships. When you can bravely acknowledge your own feelings and hold space for others' emotions, you create the conditions for genuine intimacy and connection. You communicate more openly and honestly, leading to greater understanding and trust. You're also better equipped to navigate conflicts or difficult conversations with grace and skill.

In the workplace, emotional agility is a key driver of success, particularly in fast-paced, high-pressure, or ambiguous environments. Leaders and employees who can deftly manage their own emotions are more adaptable, proactive, and solution-focused. They bounce back quicker from setbacks, take more calculated risks, and perform better under stress. Emotional agility enables you to communicate a compelling vision, have challenging conversations, and unite and inspire others.

Another powerful benefit of emotional agility is greater self-knowledge, personal growth, and overall life satisfaction. By mindfully observing your thought patterns and emotional habits, you develop keener self-awareness and insight. This empowers you to consciously choose behaviors and responses that are adaptive and aligned with your values. Over time, you learn to author your life story and shape your experiences in a way that is meaningful and fulfilling to you.

Ultimately, emotional agility liberates you from being controlled by your thoughts, feelings, and circumstances. It provides a path to realize your fullest potential and thrive, not just in the absence of challenge but in the very midst of it. When you develop a more agile, resilient inner world, your outer world transforms in remarkable ways.

Solution #1: Logical and Critical Thinking

One of the most effective ways to build emotional agility and mental toughness is to harness the power of logical and critical thinking. When you learn to analyze situations objectively, question assumptions, and reason through problems systematically, you gain greater control over your mind and emotions. Let's explore what logical and critical thinking entails and how to cultivate these invaluable skills.

What Is Critical Thinking?

At its core, critical thinking is the ability to analyze information objectively and make a reasoned judgment. It involves looking at situations from all angles, evaluating evidence and arguments rationally, and reaching well-founded conclusions. Critical thinkers ask probing questions, challenge assumptions, and resist jumping to conclusions based on emotions or preconceived notions.

Some key traits of critical thinking include:

- questioning evidence and assumptions
- analyzing connections and patterns objectively
- reasoning through logic and weighing probabilities
- recognizing and avoiding cognitive biases
- considering alternate possibilities and perspectives
- reaching evidence-based conclusions
- communicating rationally to explain thinking

Critical thinking enables you to navigate complex situations with greater mental clarity, solve problems more effectively, and make sounder decisions aligned with your goals. When you approach challenges as a critical thinker, you build mental resilience to stay level-headed even in emotionally charged situations.

Thinking With Reason

Logical thinking is a critical component of developing emotional agility. It involves analyzing cause-and-effect relationships, recognizing patterns, and understanding the likely outcomes of different choices. By gathering relevant facts and evidence, questioning assumptions, and considering probabilities, you can draw well-founded conclusions based on reasoning rather than emotional reactivity.

To strengthen your logical thinking skills, start by cultivating a habit of gathering relevant information and data to inform your reasoning. This may include past experiences, concrete evidence, and expert insights. Next, challenge your preconceived notions and confirm that you're working with facts rather than unexamined beliefs. Look for patterns, connections, and cause-and-effect relationships between events to understand how they impact each other.

When faced with a decision or challenge, consider the probable outcomes of different actions by reasoning through "if-then" logic. Avoid the temptation to oversimplify complex issues or overlook nuance by resisting generalizations and black-and-white thinking. Instead, strive to reach reasonable conclusions that are supported by the available facts and evidence.

By routinely practicing logical thinking, you train your mind to respond rationally to stressful situations rather than getting hijacked by volatile emotions. This enables you to approach problems with mental clarity and identify optimal solutions, even in the face of adversity.

The Importance of Critical and Logical Thinking

Developing critical and logical thinking skills is essential for navigating life's challenges with emotional agility. By questioning initial assumptions, gathering relevant data, exploring alternative perspectives, and analyzing cause-and-effect relationships, you can respond intentionally rather than reactively to stressful situations.

One key aspect of critical thinking is checking for cognitive distortions—such as catastrophizing, overgeneralizing, or discounting positives—that can skew your perception of a situation. By objectively examining your thoughts and feelings, you can identify any irrational or unproductive patterns and replace them with more balanced, realistic thinking.

Logical thinking enables you to reason through possible solutions and choose a course of action most likely to generate positive outcomes. By weighing the probable consequences of different choices and reaching an objective conclusion aligned with your goals and values, you can respond effectively to any challenge.

With practice, critical and logical thinking skills become habitual, allowing you to approach stressful situations with mental toughness and resilience. By integrating lessons learned from past experiences, you continually refine your ability to navigate life's obstacles with emotional agility and grace. Ultimately, developing a rational, grounded mindset empowers you to thrive in the face of adversity and maintain emotional equilibrium, even in the most challenging circumstances.

Solution #2: Emotional Awareness

Another critical component of developing emotional agility and mental toughness is cultivating emotional awareness. When you can accurately identify and understand your own emotions, you gain valuable insight into your inner world. This self-knowledge becomes a powerful tool for managing your thoughts, feelings, and reactions more effectively.

Understanding Emotional Awareness

Emotional awareness is the ability to recognize and understand your own emotions as they occur. It involves paying attention to your inner experiences, including physical sensations, thoughts, and feelings. With high emotional awareness, you can accurately identify and name your emotions, understand their sources, and recognize how they impact your behaviors and decisions.

Some key aspects of emotional awareness include:

- noticing and naming your emotions accurately
- identifying the triggers or sources of your feelings
- recognizing how emotions impact your thoughts and behaviors
- understanding the nuances and complexities of emotions
- linking current emotions to past experiences and patterns
- anticipating potential emotional reactions to situations

When you cultivate emotional awareness, you're better able to manage your inner world proactively. You can spot emotional triggers, anticipate challenging situations, and take steps to regulate your reactions. Emotional awareness allows you to respond intentionally rather than getting derailed by unexpected or overwhelming feelings.

Tips for Emotional Awareness

Building emotional awareness is an ongoing practice that gets easier over time. Use these tips to tune into your inner world and strengthen your emotional agility:

- **Pay attention to physical sensations.** Notice changes in your body, like tightness in your chest or butterflies in your stomach, as clues to underlying emotions.
- **Identify and name your feelings specifically.** Go beyond generic labels like "good" or "bad" to pinpoint precise emotions like excited, disappointed, proud, or anxious.
- **Notice your emotional triggers.** Recognize the situations, people, or events that tend to spark specific feelings for you.
- **Explore the root causes of your reactions.** Look beneath surface-level emotions to understand the core fears, beliefs, or past experiences driving your feelings.

- **Keep an emotions journal.** Writing about your daily emotional experiences helps you process feelings and spot recurring patterns over time.
- **Tune into your self-talk.** Notice the inner dialogue impacting your emotions, like harsh self-criticism or catastrophic predictions.
- **Practice mindfulness.** Develop present-moment awareness of your thoughts and feelings through practices like meditation or deep breathing.
- **Cultivate curiosity and self-compassion.** Approach your emotions with openness and kindness rather than self-judgment.

As you build emotional awareness, you start to recognize your unique patterns of thoughts, feelings, and reactions. You discover the emotional strengths and skills that help you navigate challenges effectively, like the ability to bounce back after setbacks or stay calm under pressure. You also identify the emotional triggers or tendencies that undermine your resilience and mental toughness, like a habit of worrying or a fear of failure.

With this self-knowledge, you can focus on leveraging your emotional strengths and developing the agility skills you need to thrive. Emotional awareness becomes the foundation for effectively managing your inner world. You learn to catch problematic thoughts or emotional reactions early, implement proactive coping strategies, and consciously choose responses that align with your values and goals.

By developing emotional awareness, you build the mental toughness and flexibility to navigate life's ups and downs masterfully. You face the full depths of your emotional world with honesty, clarity, and self-compassion. Challenges become opportunities for growth and learning. No matter what arises, you have the self-knowledge and emotional agility to choose intentional responses that keep you grounded, centered, and moving forward purposefully.

Solution #3: Bouncing Back With Resilience

Emotional agility and mental toughness are ultimately about resilience—the ability to face adversity, navigate challenges, and bounce back stronger. Resilience is a key theme that we explore in depth in the book *Mastering Emotional Intelligence With Ease*. Readers who have already delved into that resource will find that the concepts and strategies discussed here build upon and complement the resilience skills covered in that book.

In *Mastering Emotional Intelligence With Ease*, we lay the foundation for understanding what resilience is and why it's so critical for emotional well-being. We explore the core components of resilience, such as self-awareness, adaptability, and a growth mindset. The book also provides practical exercises and techniques for developing these resilience skills in daily life.

Building upon that foundational knowledge, the strategies we'll explore in this section focus specifically on how resilience relates to emotional agility and mental toughness. We'll delve into targeted techniques for boosting resilience in the face of challenges and setbacks, such as reframing adversity, cultivating optimism, and practicing self-compassion. We'll also emphasize the power of social support and strong relationships in fostering resilience.

For readers who haven't yet explored *Mastering Emotional Intelligence With Ease*, that book offers a comprehensive look at the science and practice of resilience. You'll gain a deeper under-standing of the psychological factors that contribute to resilience, as well as evidence-based strategies for strengthening your ability to bounce back from setbacks. The book also provides valuable insights into how resilience intersects with other key areas of emotional intelligence, such as self-awareness, empathy, and motivation.

Whether you've already read *Mastering Emotional Intelligence With Ease* or are new to these concepts, the strategies and insights covered in this section will empower you to cultivate the resilience needed to thrive in the face of any challenge. By combining the foundational knowledge from the previous book with the targeted techniques explored here, you'll develop a comprehensive toolkit for navigating life's obstacles with emotional agility, mental tough-ness, and resilience. Let's dive in and explore practical strategies to boost your resilience and leverage the power of social support.

How to be More Resilient

Resilience is like a muscle—it can be strengthened over time with practice and persistence. Use these proven tips and techniques to build your resilience:

- **Reframe challenges as opportunities.** Look for the potential benefits or lessons in difficult situations. Adopt a growth mindset and view obstacles as chances to learn and improve.
- **Focus on what you can control.** When faced with adversity, direct your energy toward what's within your sphere of influence rather than fixating on factors beyond your control.

- **Practice self-care.** Prioritize healthy habits like proper nutrition, regular exercise, quality sleep, and stress management techniques. Taking care of your physical and emotional well-being builds resilience.
- **Cultivate a positive outlook.** Look for the good in situations and people. Practice gratitude, savor joyful moments, and maintain a hopeful perspective about the future.
- **Set realistic goals and take action.** Break challenges down into manageable steps and take consistent action toward your objectives. Celebrate your progress along the way.
- **Learn from setbacks.** When you encounter obstacles or failures, reflect on what you can learn from the experience. Identify areas for improvement and adjust your approach accordingly.
- **Nurture a strong support system.** Surround yourself with positive, supportive people who believe in you. Reach out for help and encouragement when needed.
- **Develop a sense of purpose.** Connect to your core values and life meaning. Pursue activities and goals that energize and inspire you. A strong sense of purpose fuels resilience.

By incorporating these strategies into your life, you train your mind and emotions to be more resilient. You develop the agility and grit to face any challenge head-on, knowing that you have the inner resources to cope effectively and emerge stronger.

Finding Support in Others

One of the most powerful ways to boost resilience is to cultivate a strong support system. Connecting with others provides a vital source of encouragement, guidance, and practical help during tough times. When you have people you can count on, you're better able to weather any storm.

To build a resilient support network:

- **Identify your support squad.** Make a list of the people in your life who are positive, reliable, and encouraging. Consider family, friends, colleagues, mentors, or professionals like counselors or coaches.
- **Nurture your relationships.** Invest time and energy into building strong, healthy connections with your support people. Show up for them during their challenging times, too.
- **Communicate openly and honestly.** Share your struggles, fears, and goals with trusted confidantes. Allow yourself to be vulnerable and ask for help when needed.
- **Seek out role models and mentors.** Connect with people who have navigated challenges similar to your own. Learn from their experiences and insights.
- **Join supportive communities.** Participate in groups or organizations aligned with your values and interests, where you can find a sense of belonging and shared purpose.
- **Offer support to others.** Providing encouragement and assistance to others facing tough times not only helps them but also boosts your own resilience and sense of meaning.

Remember, resilience isn't about facing challenges alone or being completely self-reliant. It's about knowing when to lean on others and being willing to accept support. By surrounding yourself with caring, encouraging people, you create a powerful buffer against life's storms. You're reminded that you aren't alone, that you're valued and believed in.

Ultimately, emotional agility, mental toughness, and resilience are interconnected skills that empower you to face any challenge with confidence and grace. By developing self-awareness, critical thinking abilities, and a supportive network, you cultivate the inner strength to overcome obstacles and create the life you envision. No matter what arises, you trust in your ability to feel your emotions fully, respond intentionally, and continue moving forward with purpose and conviction.

Wrapping Up...

In this chapter, we explored emotional agility, uncovering its impact on cultivating mental toughness and resilience. By honing the skills to consciously and intentionally navigate your emotional landscape, you gain the flexibility and inner strength to thrive in the face of any challenge.

Throughout this chapter, we've covered essential strategies for honing our emotional agility, including:

- Harnessing logical and critical thinking, analyzing situations objectively, questioning assumptions, reasoning through problems systematically, and reaching evidence-based conclusions before reacting emotionally.
- Cultivating emotional awareness, tuning into your inner world, accurately identifying and understanding your emotions, recognizing triggers and patterns, and exploring the root causes and impacts of your feelings.
- Building resilience, reframing challenges as opportunities, focusing on what you can control, cultivating a positive outlook, learning from setbacks, and leaning on a strong support system to bounce back stronger from adversity.

Emotional agility is a critical component of mental toughness, empowering you to harness the insights and energy of your emotions rather than being controlled by them. By developing self-mastery and emotional intelligence, you'll be equipped to navigate change, uncertainty, and adversity with unwavering inner calm and resolve.

As we continue our journey toward unbreakable mental strength, the next chapter will take us into the realm of authentic confidence and self-assuredness. We'll explore powerful strategies for rewriting limiting beliefs, upgrading your identity, and boldly stepping into your full potential. Get ready to experience the unstoppable force of true confidence combined with emotional agility as you unleash your inner power and resilience in every aspect of your life.

Case Study: Kristin

Kristin, a 35-year-old marketing executive, had always prided herself on her ability to handle high-pressure situations at work. However, when she was passed over for a promotion she had been working toward for years, she found herself struggling to cope with the overwhelming emotions that followed.

Feeling a mix of anger, disappointment, and self-doubt, Kristin initially tried to suppress her emotions and push through her daily responsibilities. She told herself that she needed to be mentally tough and that these feelings were a sign of weakness. However, as the weeks passed, she found herself becoming more irritable, less focused, and increasingly disengaged from her work and personal life.

Recognizing that her current approach wasn't serving her, Kristin decided to seek guidance from a coach specializing in emotional intelligence and resilience. Through her work with the coach, Kristin began to understand the importance of emotional agility in maintaining mental toughness.

She learned to

- acknowledge and accept her emotions without judgment, recognizing that they were valid responses to a challenging situation.
- practice mindfulness to observe her thoughts and feelings without getting caught up in them, creating space for clarity and intentional action.
- challenge her assumptions and reframe her perspective, looking for opportunities for growth and learning in the face of adversity.
- cultivate self-compassion, treating herself with kindness and understanding rather than harsh self-criticism.
- develop a proactive resilience plan, identifying her strengths, support systems, and coping strategies to navigate future challenges.

As Kristin began to incorporate these emotional agility practices into her daily life, she noticed a significant shift in her mindset and well-being. Rather than feeling overwhelmed and controlled by her emotions, she developed the flexibility and resilience to navigate her inner world with greater ease and intention.

With her newfound emotional agility, Kristin was able to approach her work with renewed focus and motivation. She started to view the missed promotion as an opportunity to reassess her career goals and develop new skills. She also became a more supportive and understanding leader for her team, creating a culture of openness and resilience in the face of challenges.

Kristin's journey to emotional agility not only transformed her ability to cope with the disappointment of the missed promotion but also equipped her with the inner strength and flexibility to thrive in the face of future adversities. By embracing her emotions as valuable sources of insight and learning, Kristin discovered that true mental toughness lay in her ability to adapt, grow, and move forward with intention and grace.

Encourage Others to Listen to Their Emotions

"The human capacity for burden is like bamboo — far more flexible than you'd ever believe at first glance."

Jodi Picoult

Earlier in this book, I shared the story of Kate — a woman who had lost her job and thought her world would fall apart, only to discover her immense resilience. The first step toward her progress lay in recognizing the full gamut of her emotions, including sadness about having invested so much in an employer who no longer had a place for her, and worry about her future financial stability.

Vulnerability is a buzzword on the current mental health and wellness scene, but it's just the tip of the iceberg. Embracing your imperfection, asking for support, and taking risks are all key components of resilience, but so, too, is listening to your emotions.

Anger, fear, sadness, disappointment… these are all powerful signs that it's time to make much-needed changes. Within the discomfort and pain they bring lie the kernels of change. Resilience isn't about putting on a brave face and hiding what we feel. Quite the opposite. It's about feeling emotion, understanding that challenges are what make us grow, and pushing through the pain.

I hope that by this stage in your reading, you have seen how big life changes and obstacles can lead you to positive choices such as embracing mindfulness, managing stress proactively, and honing your mental agility. If the strategies in this book have made a difference in your life, then you're in the perfect position to help someone else.

By leaving a review on Amazon, you'll help other readers discover the key steps they need to take to move beyond life's biggest setbacks.

Share your opinion of this book and a little bit about your own story. One of the most powerful ways to boost your own strength is to help others hone theirs.

Thank you for your support. Together, we can shine the light on the transformative power of our thoughts and emotions.

Scan the QR code

FIVE

Step #4—Skyrocket Your Confidence

> *You never know how strong you are, until being strong is your only choice.*
>
> Bob Marley

S elf-doubt. Imposter syndrome. Negative self-talk. We've all experienced those confidence-draining thoughts that make us question our abilities and self-worth. But here's the truth: Confidence isn't just a feel-good emotion—it's a crucial ingredient in the recipe for mental toughness. When you believe in yourself and your capabilities, you're far more likely to persevere in the face of challenges and bounce back from setbacks.

In this chapter, we'll unpack what genuine confidence looks like, why it's so vital for a resilient mindset, and practical strategies you can start implementing today to boost your self-assurance. Get ready to begin seeing yourself in a whole new light!

The Value of Confidence

So, what exactly do we mean by confidence? In essence, confidence is a feeling of trust in your qualities, abilities, and judgment. It's an inner knowing that you're capable of handling what life throws at you. Confident people exude a sense of calm self-assurance and are willing to take risks, seize opportunities, and stand up for what they believe in.

But make no mistake—confidence isn't about being immune to fear or never experiencing self-doubt. Even the most self-assured among us have moments when we second-guess ourselves. The difference lies in not allowing those doubts to paralyze or hold you back from going after what you want.

Why is confidence so crucial for mental toughness? For starters, confidence empowers you to step outside your comfort zone. When you have faith in your abilities, you're more likely to take on new challenges, pursue ambitious goals, and embrace the discomfort that comes with growth and learning.

Additionally, confidence helps you maintain perspective and reframe obstacles as opportunities. Rather than being derailed by setbacks, a confident mindset enables you to extract valuable lessons from failures and keep moving forward. You're also better equipped to advocate for yourself, set healthy boundaries, and make self-honoring choices.

Common Barriers to Confidence

If self-confidence is so important, why do so many of us struggle with it? The reality is that there are numerous barriers that can chip away at even the heartiest of self-esteem. Some common confidence killers include:

- **Perfectionism and fear of failure.** When you equate your worth with flawless performance, the pressure to "get it right" can be paralyzing.
- **Comparison and competition.** In our social-media saturated world, it's easy to fall into the trap of measuring yourself against curated highlight reels and feeling like you're falling short.
- **Lack of self-compassion.** Confident people aren't immune to inner critics, but they know how to respond to themselves with kindness and understanding rather than harsh judgment.
- **Scarcity mindset.** If you're prone to "never enough" thinking, you may have trouble internalizing your accomplishments and valuing what you bring to the table.

If any of these barriers resonate with you, take heart in knowing that confidence is not a fixed trait but a skill that can be cultivated and strengthened.

Solution #1: Celebrate the Small Things

One of the simplest yet most impactful ways to skyrocket your confidence is to start acknowledging your wins, however small they may seem. By celebrating minor milestones and accomplishments, you gradually build a reservoir of positive evidence that boosts your self-assurance.

Why Celebrating Small Victories Matters

When you get in the habit of recognizing your daily efforts and achievements, you train your brain to focus on success rather than dwelling on shortcomings. This shift in perspective is crucial for cultivating a resilient, confident mindset.

Celebrating small wins also helps counteract the negative bias that often plagues our self-perception. Our brains are wired to pay more attention to failures and mistakes than to successes and triumphs. By intentionally highlighting your victories, you create a more balanced and accurate view of your abilities.

Moreover, acknowledging minor milestones provides a steady stream of motivation and encouragement. When you take the time to savor your progress, you're more likely to stay engaged and persistent in the face of challenges. Each small win becomes a building block of confidence, propelling you forward.

How to Make It a Habit

To start harnessing the power of small victories, try implementing these simple practices:

- **Keep a daily success log:** At the end of each day, write down three things you accomplished or handled well. These don't have to be monumental feats—simply cooking a nourishing meal or tackling a dreaded email counts.
- **Share your wins with others:** Don't be afraid to celebrate your successes with supportive friends, family, or colleagues. Their recognition and encouragement can further bolster your confidence.
- **Savor the moment:** When you achieve a goal or milestone, take a few minutes to fully appreciate the experience. Notice how it feels in your body and mind to have succeeded.
- **Reframe challenges as opportunities:** When faced with a difficult task or situation, ask yourself, "How can I break this down into manageable steps and create small wins along the way?"

By consistently celebrating your small victories, you'll develop a more confident, resilient mindset. You'll start to notice and appreciate your strengths, skills, and accomplishments, creating a positive feedback loop that fuels further success.

Solution #2: Hone a Growth Mindset

The way you think about skills and abilities has a huge impact on your confidence levels. Cultivating a growth mindset—the belief that you can improve and expand your abilities through effort and learning—is a game-changer for building self-assurance.

Fixed vs. Growth: Two Ways of Thinking

While the concepts of fixed and growth mindsets are discussed briefly in *Mastering Emotional Intelligence With Ease*, they also have significant relevance to developing mental toughness. According to research by psychologist Carol Dweck, people generally fall into two camps when it comes to their beliefs about ability: those with a fixed mindset and those with a growth mindset (2012).

If you have a fixed mindset, you tend to view talents and intelligence as static, unchangeable traits. You believe that you're either naturally good at something or you're not. With this perspective, challenges and setbacks become threats to your sense of competence and worth.

In contrast, a growth mindset sees skills and abilities as malleable qualities that can be developed over time. If you have a growth orientation, you view challenges as opportunities to learn and improve. Mistakes and failures aren't indicative of a lack of talent but rather stepping stones to mastery.

Benefits of a Growth Mindset

Adopting a growth mindset is a powerful way to enhance your confidence and resilience. When you trust in your capacity to learn and grow, you're less likely to be derailed by self-doubt or fear of failure.

A growth mindset also fosters a healthier relationship with risk-taking and setbacks. Instead of shying away from challenges or beating yourself up over mistakes, you embrace difficulty as a chance to stretch beyond your comfort zone. You view failure as feedback to learn from rather than a judgment of your worth.

Furthermore, a growth mindset allows you to find inspiration in the success of others rather than feeling threatened or discouraged by their accomplishments. You recognize that their triumphs are proof of what's possible through dedication and effort.

Cultivating a Growth-Oriented Mindset

To start shifting from a fixed to a growth mindset, try implementing these practices:

- **Embrace the power of "yet":** When you catch yourself thinking, *I'm not good at this*, add the word "yet" to the end of the sentence. Remind yourself that your current abilities aren't fixed or final.
- **Reframe challenges as learning opportunities:** When faced with a difficult task or situation, ask yourself, "What can I learn from this?" instead of "What if I fail?"
- **Celebrate effort and progress, not just results:** Recognize the hard work and strategies that go into your successes, not just the end outcome. Focus on the process of growth rather than fixating on perfection.

- **Learn from the successes of others:** When you witness someone else thriving, get curious about their journey. What mindsets and practices have they cultivated to reach that point? Use their example as inspiration and proof of what's possible.

By consciously shifting toward a growth mindset, you'll develop unshakable confidence in your ability to learn, improve, and achieve your goals. Setbacks and challenges will become stepping stones to success rather than threats to your sense of self. You'll approach life with a newfound sense of curiosity, resilience, and self-assurance.

Solution #3: Engage

One of the most powerful ways to supercharge your confidence is to take a proactive stance in your life. Confidence is ultimately a result of doing, learning, and growing—not just thinking or preparing. By embracing challenges and new experiences, you'll cultivate an unshakable trust in your abilities.

Engagement: The Key to Confidence

It's easy to fall into the trap of "analysis paralysis"—endlessly researching, planning, and ruminating rather than actually diving in. But true confidence emerges from putting yourself out there and engaging with life wholeheartedly.

When you take bold action, even in the face of fear or uncertainty, you send a powerful message to your subconscious mind. You affirm your belief in your ability to handle challenges and navigate new terrain. Each courageous step reinforces the notion that you are capable, competent, and resilient.

Moreover, taking action allows you to gather real-world evidence of your abilities. As you tackle new challenges and learn from your experiences, you'll develop a robust sense of self-efficacy—the belief in your capacity to succeed. This self-trust is the foundation of unshakeable confidence.

Strategies for Bold Engagement

To start building your confidence through courageous action, try these strategies:

- **Pursue flow-inducing hobbies:** Engage in activities that fully absorb your attention and allow you to lose yourself in the process. These "flow states" provide a powerful boost of confidence and self-assurance.
- **Set stretch goals:** Challenge yourself to step outside your comfort zone regularly. Set ambitious goals that require you to grow and expand your skills. Remember, the aim isn't perfection but rather consistent progress.
- **Embrace discomfort:** Recognize that feeling uncomfortable is often a sign that you're growing and learning. Lean into that discomfort and view it as a positive signal that you're becoming more confident and capable.
- **Learn voraciously:** Continuously seek out opportunities to gain knowledge and sharpen your abilities. Read books, attend workshops, seek mentorship—immerse yourself in the process of self-improvement.
- **Fail forward:** Reframe failures and setbacks as valuable learning experiences. Instead of letting them shake your confidence, view them as stepping stones to mastery. Cultivate the resilience to bounce back and keep moving forward.

By consistently taking bold, courageous action, you'll cultivate a strong sense of confidence and self-assurance. You'll develop a deep trust in your ability to handle whatever challenges come your way, knowing that each experience is an opportunity to learn, grow, and become the best version of yourself.

Wrapping Up...

In this chapter, we delved into the transformative power of confidence in cultivating mental toughness. By recognizing the immense value of self-assurance and implementing practical strategies to boost your confidence, you lay the foundation for unshakable resilience in the face of any challenge.

We've explored a range of essential techniques to boost your confidence, including:

- embracing a growth mindset to view challenges as opportunities for learning and improvement
- celebrating small victories to build a reservoir of positive evidence and boost self-assurance
- engaging in flow-inducing hobbies and setting stretch goals to build confidence through courageous action

Confidence is the fuel that propels you forward, empowering you to take bold action, seize opportunities, and bounce back from setbacks with renewed determination. By cultivating an unshakable belief in your abilities and potential, you'll be equipped to tackle even the most daunting challenges head-on.

As we continue our exploration of mental toughness, the next chapter will invite us to take control of one of our most precious resources: time. We'll dive into game-changing strategies for mastering productivity, prioritizing your goals, and designing a life that truly lights you up. Get ready to shift from a reactive to a proactive mindset as you learn to make every moment count and achieve your wildest dreams with unwavering focus and efficiency.

Case Study: Robert

Robert, a 48-year-old high school teacher, had always been passionate about education and making a difference in his students' lives. However, despite his years of experience and dedication to his craft, Robert often found himself plagued by self-doubt and a nagging sense that he wasn't truly making an impact.

As he watched younger, more tech-savvy teachers join the faculty and effortlessly connect with students, Robert began to question his own abilities and relevance. He shied away from taking on new initiatives or speaking up in faculty meetings, fearing that his ideas were outdated or unworthy of consideration.

Recognizing that his lack of confidence was not only impacting his professional growth but also his ability to be the best possible educator for his students, Robert resolved to take action. He started by exploring the root causes of his self-doubt, tracing it back to a deeply ingrained belief that he was "too old to learn new tricks" and a tendency to compare himself unfavorably to his colleagues.

Armed with this self-awareness, Robert embarked on a journey to rebuild his confidence from the inside out. He began by celebrating the small victories in his classroom each day, whether it was a student's "aha" moment during a lesson or a heartfelt thank-you from a graduating senior. These moments served as powerful reminders of his impact and value as an educator.

Robert also made a conscious effort to adopt a growth mindset, viewing challenges and setbacks as opportunities for learning and development. He enrolled in professional development workshops to expand his skill set, particularly in areas like technology integration and student-centered learning. As he stepped outside his comfort zone and acquired new knowledge, Robert began to see himself as a lifelong learner rather than someone whose best days were behind him.

To further boost his confidence, Robert sought out a mentor in the form of a veteran teacher who had successfully navigated the evolving landscape of education. This mentor provided guidance, support, and encouragement as Robert took on new challenges and explored innovative teaching strategies.

Alongside these efforts, Robert reconnected with his love for hiking and nature photography, hobbies that had fallen by the wayside in the busyness of life. He carved out time each weekend to hit the trails, finding solace and renewal in the great outdoors. As he immersed himself in these confidence-fueling pursuits, Robert found his sense of self-assurance and resilience spilled over into his teaching.

Gradually, Robert began to notice a profound shift in his mindset and presence in the classroom. He approached his lessons with newfound enthusiasm and creativity, unafraid to take risks and try new approaches. His students responded to his renewed energy and confidence, leading to deeper engagement and more meaningful learning experiences.

Perhaps most significantly, Robert learned to silence his inner critic and embrace his unique strengths as an educator. He came to understand that his experience, wisdom, and dedication were invaluable assets and that he had the power to continue making a profound difference in his students' lives.

Through his journey, Robert discovered that confidence is not about being perfect or having all the answers but rather about trusting in one's ability to learn, grow, and make a meaningful impact. By combining practical strategies like celebrating small wins, embracing a growth mindset, seeking out mentorship, and engaging in fulfilling hobbies, he was able to rewrite his internal narrative and tap into his full potential as an educator.

Robert's story serves as a powerful reminder that it's never too late to invest in oneself and cultivate unshakable confidence. His journey highlights that true mental toughness is not about the absence of fear or doubt but rather the resilience and self-belief to keep moving forward in the pursuit of one's passions and purpose.

SIX

Step #5—Time is Ticking... Better Manage It!

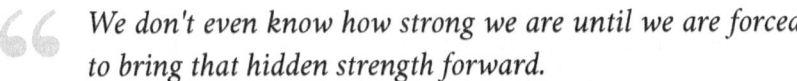 *We don't even know how strong we are until we are forced to bring that hidden strength forward.*

Isabel Allende

Do you constantly feel like there aren't enough hours in the day? Like no matter how hard you try, you just can't seem to get a handle on your time and responsibilities? If so, you're far from alone. In today's fast-paced world, poor time management is one of the most common barriers to achieving mental toughness and resilience.

When we allow time to slip through our fingers, it leads to missed deadlines, forgotten commitments, and a perpetual state of feeling overwhelmed. This chronic stress erodes our confidence and inner strength. Pretty soon, we feel totally out of control, helplessly adrift in a chaotic sea of obligations and unfinished business.

But here's the good news—it doesn't have to be this way. With the right time management strategies, you can take back the reins, reduce your stress levels, and build the mental fortitude to handle whatever life throws your way. In this chapter, I'll share some of the most effective techniques for mastering your minutes and harnessing your hours. Get ready to feel empowered, productive, and mentally tough!

The Time Management Tango

What exactly do we mean by "time management" anyway? At its core, time management is the process of organizing and planning how to allocate your hours to specific activities. It's about working smarter, not harder, to achieve maximum productivity and minimum stress, especially when deadlines are tight and pressures are high.

Time management is a skill that involves goal setting, planning, prioritizing, and controlling how much time you spend on specific tasks. It's about using your time wisely and efficiently to achieve your goals and reach your full potential. Good time management allows you to work smarter, not harder, so you can get more done in less time, even when pressures are high.

Signs of effective time management include:

- prioritizing important tasks
- meeting deadlines consistently
- feeling in control of your schedule
- having time for strategic planning
- maintaining work–life balance
- staying focused with minimal distractions
- delegating when appropriate
- communicating timelines clearly

In contrast, poor time managers tend to:

- miss deadlines frequently
- procrastinate on important projects
- feel perpetually stressed and overwhelmed
- neglect planning and work reactively instead
- struggle with work–life boundaries
- get sidetracked by low-priority interruptions
- hoard tasks rather than delegating
- overpromise and underdeliver

Effective time management is crucial for achieving goals, reducing stress, and improving overall quality of life. When you have good time management skills, you feel more in control of your day, leading to lower stress levels and improved mental well-being. This enables you to be more productive and efficient, produce higher quality work, make better decisions, and have more free time for hobbies and relationships. As a result, you feel more accomplished and satisfied, experience less burnout and fatigue, and can adapt to changes and unexpected events more easily. Ultimately, effective time management helps you achieve long-term goals and career advancement.

Conversely, poor time management can lead to missed deadlines, subpar work quality, strained relationships, chronic stress, and diminished mental toughness. When you're constantly behind the eight ball, it's hard to muster the resilience to bounce back from setbacks.

As you can see, stellar time management offers incredible benefits for your well-being and performance. When you're in the driver's seat of your day, you feel calmer, more competent, and more resilient overall. You're able to be proactive rather than reactive, which is a hallmark of mental toughness.

242 • AMBER PRESTON

In short, mastering time management is a major key to unlocking your inner strength and weathering life's storms. So, let's dive into some practical solutions you can implement to hone your skills.

Solution #1: Prioritization

Not all tasks are created equal. To manage your time effectively, you need to get crystal clear on your highest priorities and tackle those first. When everything feels urgent, prioritization provides a roadmap through the overwhelm. By taking decisive action on your most important activities, you build momentum, motivation, and mental muscle.

Prioritizing tasks means evaluating their importance and urgency and then ranking them in order of priority. When you prioritize effectively, you focus your time and energy on the most critical and valuable tasks, rather than getting bogged down in busywork or distractions.

Prioritizing offers numerous benefits, including improved focus and concentration, greater efficiency and productivity, enhanced decision-making abilities, reduced stress and anxiety, and an increased sense of control and accomplishment. By prioritizing, you create more time for important goals and relationships while developing the ability to adapt to changing circumstances.

There are several frameworks you can use to determine your priorities:

- **The Eisenhower Matrix:** This classic tool helps you sort tasks into four boxes based on urgency and importance:

    - Urgent and Important: Do these tasks immediately
    - Not Urgent but Important: Schedule these tasks

○ Urgent but Not Important: Delegate these tasks

○ Not Urgent and Not Important: Delete these tasks

- **RICE:** This acronym stands for Reach, Impact, Confidence, and Effort. Score tasks on a scale of 1–10 in each of these areas. Tasks with the highest total score become your top priorities.

- **ABCDE Method:** Start by making a master list of everything on your plate. Then, assign each task a letter:

   ○ A: Tasks you must do—serious consequences if not completed

   ○ B: Tasks you should do—mild consequences if not completed

   ○ C: Tasks that would be nice to do but have no consequences if not completed

   ○ D: Tasks that can be delegated to someone else

   ○ E: Tasks that can be eliminated entirely

The key to making any of these methods work is consistency. Make prioritization a daily habit, ideally at the start of each day or the night before. Ask yourself: What are the most important things I need to accomplish today? This week? This month? Then, align your time and attention accordingly.

It can also be helpful to use visual cues, like highlighting or starring top priorities in your planner or task list. The more front-of-mind your high-impact activities are, the less likely you are to get sidetracked by shiny distractions.

Remember, saying yes to one thing means saying no to something else. Be judicious about what you allow onto your plate, and be willing to let go of tasks that don't align with your highest goals and values. Mentally tough people know that focus and follow-through beat running around like a chicken with your head cut off any day.

Solution #2: Planning and Strategies

Once you're clear on your priorities, it's time to translate them into a well-crafted plan. Mentally tough people understand the necessity of preparation and strategy. As the old adage goes, "failing to plan is planning to fail."

Planning is the process of charting out the specific actions needed to achieve a goal. It involves breaking down a large project into smaller, manageable steps, setting deadlines, and identifying any resources or support you'll need along the way.

Effective planning offers several key benefits:

- provides clarity and direction
- improves efficiency and productivity
- reduces stress and anxiety
- increases chances of success
- allows for better resource allocation
- facilitates communication and collaboration
- enables course correction when needed

Here are some of the most effective time management planning strategies to build into your routine:

Time blocking: This technique involves dividing your day into distinct blocks of time, each dedicated to a specific activity. For example, you might block off 9–10 a.m. for strategic planning, 10 a.m.–12 p.m. for focused work on a high-priority project, 12 p.m.–1 p.m. for lunch and movement, 1–2 p.m. for meetings, and so on.

Time blocking combats our tendency to work reactively and get thrown off course by interruptions. It creates hard edges in your schedule, ensuring meaningful progress on your most important tasks. To make it work:

- Identify your high-priority tasks and estimate how long they'll take.
- Group similar activities together (e.g., all your calls or errands).
- Build in buffer time for the unexpected.
- Communicate your availability to others.
- Honor your blocks as non-negotiable appointments.

Using a planner: Don't try to juggle everything in your head. Invest in a physical or digital planning tool where you can capture tasks, appointments, deadlines, and ideas. Putting pen to paper clears mental clutter and helps you feel grounded.

When selecting a planner, consider:

- format (daily, weekly, monthly)
- size and portability
- customization options
- goal-setting and review pages
- bonus features like habit trackers or gratitude prompts

Each night, take a few minutes to review the day ahead. Ask yourself: What are my top three priorities? What might trip me up, and how can I stay on track? A little bit of intention goes a long way.

To-do lists: In addition to time blocking, maintain a running log of tasks on deck. But rather than throwing everything on one giant list, separate tasks into a few key categories:

- Master list: Capture everything swirling in your head in one place.
- Daily list: Pull a handful of items from your Master List to tackle today.
- Priority list: Note your top 1–3 most critical/valuable tasks.

You can also segment lists by project, timeframe (e.g., this week vs. next), or type (e.g., calls to make, errands to run). The key is to have a go-to reference for staying organized and focused.

To make your lists work for you:

- Keep them short and realistic—aim for 3–5 items per day.
- Use actionable language (e.g., "Draft proposal" vs. "Work on proposal").
- Assign due dates and estimate the time needed.
- Cross off completed items for a sense of progress.
- Review and update regularly.

Again, prioritization is paramount. Always highlight your top three to-dos and weigh those most heavily. Don't fall into the trap of confusing being busy with being productive.

Planning and preparation are key ingredients in the recipe for mental toughness. When you take the time to chart your course, anticipate obstacles, and build in contingencies, you feel more capable and in control. You're able to weather life's curveballs with greater equanimity because you have a clear sense of direction and purpose.

Solution #3: Letting Go of the Extra

Even the best-laid plans can go awry if you're drowning in excess. Mentally tough people know that addition by subtraction is a real thing. Lightening your load is a prerequisite to following through on what matters most.

Overcommitting is a common trap that can sabotage even the most well-intentioned time management efforts. When you try to do too much, you end up doing nothing well. You're spread thin, stressed out, and unable to give your full focus and energy to your highest priorities.

Learning to let go of extraneous responsibilities and obligations is a critical skill for boosting mental strength and resilience. It allows you to reclaim your time, attention, and energy for the things that truly matter to you.

Here's how to start identifying what commitments or obligations you may need to release:

1. Write down everything currently on your plate (work projects, side hustles, volunteer roles, committees, social clubs, etc.).
2. Give each a score from 1–10 based on (a) how much you enjoy it and (b) how much it contributes to your highest goals/values.
3. Highlight any items with a combined score of less than 10.
4. Ask yourself: What would happen if I didn't do this anymore? What's the worst case scenario? The best case?
5. Notice any fears or limiting beliefs that arise (e.g., "I don't want to let anyone down" or "I'm not allowed to say no").
6. Start with the lowest-scored item and take one small step to release or reduce that commitment.

This process can be challenging, especially if you're used to being the go-to person or pride yourself on having a full plate. But remember, every time you say "yes" to something, you're saying "no" to something else—including your precious time and energy.

Some strategies that can help ease the transition:

- Look for opportunities to delegate, automate, or simplify before eliminating altogether.
- Communicate proactively about changes to set expectations and avoid dropping the ball.
- Offer alternative resources or solutions when you do say no.
- Practice self-compassion—releasing something doesn't make you a failure or flake.
- Focus forward on what you're saying YES to (more whitespace, more buckets filled).

Mentally strong people understand that doing less can often mean accomplishing more. They're willing to make tough choices about where to invest their resources, even if it means disappointing others in the short term. They know that creating space for what matters most is the path to fulfillment and inner peace.

Wrapping Up...

We've covered a lot of ground in this chapter. To recap, time management is a critical skill for cultivating mental toughness and resilience. When you're at the mercy of your calendar, everything feels harder. But when you take charge of your days with intentionality and strategy, you tap into deep wells of inner power and poise.

The three keys to stellar time management are:

- **Prioritization:** Getting crystal clear on what matters most and tackling those items first
- **Planning:** Implementing proven strategies like time blocking and list-making to stay organized and on track
- **Pruning:** Letting go of extraneous commitments to free up bandwidth for your highest-impact activities

With these tools in hand, you're well on your way to feeling grounded, empowered, and in control no matter what life brings your way. You'll be able to meet challenges with greater confidence and equanimity, knowing that you're focused on what truly matters.

But time management is just one piece of the mental toughness puzzle. In the next chapter, we'll dive into another critical component: the art of setting and upholding healthy boundaries. Get ready to communicate your needs with clarity and conviction so you can stay true to yourself in the face of life's demands.

Case Study: Erika

Erika was a busy marketing manager who constantly felt overwhelmed and stressed out. Despite working long hours and weekends, she always seemed to be behind on her deadlines and commitments. Her work quality was suffering, and she had little time or energy left for her personal life and relationships.

One day, Erika reached a breaking point. She knew something had to change if she wanted to regain control of her life and build the mental resilience to handle her demanding career. She decided to seek out a time management coach to help her develop new skills and strategies.

The first thing Erika's coach had her do was a time audit. For one week, Erika tracked how she spent every minute of her day, from the moment she woke up until she went to bed. The results were eye-opening. Erika realized she was wasting hours each day on low-priority tasks, distractions, and interruptions. She was constantly reacting to other people's demands rather than proactively focusing on her own goals and priorities.

Armed with this insight, Erika and her coach set about creating a new time management plan. They started by clarifying Erika's top priorities and values, both at work and in her personal life. Erika realized that she had been neglecting her health, relationships, and creative passions in favor of work demands that often weren't even that important.

Next, Erika learned how to use the Eisenhower Matrix to categorize her tasks based on urgency and importance. She committed to spending the majority of her time on important but not urgent activities like strategic planning, skill development, and relationship building. She also set boundaries around her availability, communicating to her team when she would be working on focused solo tasks and when she was available for meetings and collaboration.

Erika also implemented time blocking to create dedicated chunks of time for different types of activities. She blocked off her mornings for deep work on her highest priority projects, her afternoons for meetings and administrative tasks, and her evenings for exercise, family time, and hobbies. She used a digital calendar to schedule these blocks and communicated her plan to her team and family.

To stay organized and on track, Erika started using a bullet journal to capture and prioritize her daily and weekly tasks. She also conducted a weekly review to celebrate her accomplishments, identify areas for improvement, and plan for the week ahead.

Finally, Erika took a hard look at her commitments and started practicing the art of saying no. She realized she had been over-committing out of a sense of guilt and a desire to please others. But by being more selective about what she took on, she was able to create more space for the things that truly mattered to her.

As Erika implemented these new strategies, she started to see significant improvements in her productivity, stress levels, and overall well-being. She was able to meet her deadlines with less rushing and cramming, and she had more time and energy for her personal life. She felt more in control and mentally strong, even when faced with challenging projects or tight turnarounds.

Perhaps most importantly, Erika's newfound time mastery allowed her to be more strategic and proactive in her career. Instead of just reacting to the demands of her job, she was able to carve out time for big-picture thinking, professional development, and building strong relationships with her team and stakeholders. She even started a passion project on the side, something she never would have had the bandwidth for before.

Through her journey, Erika learned that time management isn't just about being more efficient or productive. It's about aligning your time and energy with your deepest values and priorities. It's about creating a life that feels meaningful, fulfilling, and mentally strong. And while it takes effort and discipline, the payoff is more than worth it.

SEVEN

Step #6—Forming Boundaries (and Helping Them Stick)

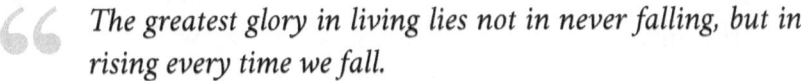 *The greatest glory in living lies not in never falling, but in rising every time we fall.*

Nelson Mandela

I magine a life without boundaries—a life where you say yes to every request, take on more than you can handle, and let others dictate your time and energy. Sounds exhausting, doesn't it? That's because it is. Living without clear boundaries is a surefire recipe for stress, resentment, and burnout. It's like having a beautiful garden with no fence to protect it from trampling feet and hungry critters. Pretty soon, your inner landscape is a mess of overturned soil and wilted blooms.

But here's the good news: Setting and maintaining healthy boundaries is a skill that anyone can learn. And it's a skill that's absolutely essential for cultivating mental toughness and resilience. When you know your limits and communicate them clearly, you create the space and safety you need to thrive. You're able to focus your energy on what matters most without getting sidetracked by other people's agendas or expectations.

In this chapter, we'll explore the power of boundaries in depth. You'll learn what boundaries are, why they're so important, and how to identify and set your own. We'll also cover strategies for communicating your boundaries with kindness and clarity, even in the face of pushback or resistance. By the end, you'll have a toolbox full of techniques for creating and sustaining the boundaries you need to be your best self. Let's dive in!

Everyone Needs Boundaries

So what exactly are boundaries, anyway? Put simply, boundaries are the limits we set to protect our time, energy, and well-being. They're the invisible lines that define what we will and won't accept in our relationships and interactions with others.

Think of boundaries like the walls of a castle. They provide structure, security, and a clear delineation between what's inside (your priorities, values, and needs) and what's outside (other people's demands and expectations). Just like a castle needs strong walls to withstand siege and invasion, you need solid boundaries to maintain your mental and emotional fortitude.

Some common examples of personal boundaries include:

- saying no to requests that don't align with your goals or values
- asking others not to comment on your appearance or weight
- limiting the amount of time you spend on social media or responding to emails outside of work hours

- declining invitations to events or activities that don't interest you or fit your schedule
- requesting that people respect your privacy and personal space
- communicating your needs and expectations clearly in relationships
- taking time for self-care and solitude without feeling guilty

At their core, boundaries are about honoring your own needs and desires. They're a way of saying "this is what works for me" and "this is what doesn't." By setting clear boundaries, you teach others how to treat you and show up for yourself with authenticity and integrity.

Boundaries are also crucial for maintaining healthy relationships. When everyone knows where they stand and what's expected of them, there's less room for misunderstanding, resentment, and conflict. Boundaries create a sense of safety and trust that allows intimacy and connection to flourish.

But perhaps most importantly, boundaries are essential for cultivating mental toughness and resilience. When you have strong boundaries in place, you're less likely to take on other people's stress or get caught up in drama that's not yours to solve. You're able to stay focused on your own goals and priorities, even in the face of outside pressure or distractions.

Boundaries also help you build self-respect and confidence. When you honor your own limits and needs, you send a powerful message to yourself and others that you matter. You reinforce the belief that your time, energy, and well-being are valuable and deserving of protection.

Without clear boundaries, it's all too easy to get swept up in other people's agendas and lose sight of your own. You may find yourself saying yes when you really want to say no, taking on more than you can handle, or sacrificing your own needs for the sake of others. Over time, this can lead to feelings of resentment, exhaustion, and even burnout.

But with strong boundaries in place, you create a buffer against the chaos and demands of the world. You're able to stay grounded in your own truth and make choices that align with your deepest values and desires. You're able to weather life's storms with greater ease and resilience because you know where you stand and what you stand for.

Of course, setting and maintaining boundaries is often easier said than done. Many of us have been conditioned from a young age to be accommodating, self-sacrificing, and "nice." We may worry that setting boundaries will make us seem selfish or uncaring or that we'll face backlash or rejection if we say no.

But the truth is, setting boundaries is one of the most caring things you can do—for yourself and for others. When you're clear about your limits and needs, you create the conditions for genuine, mutually satisfying relationships. You teach others how to respect and value you, and you model healthy self-care and self-advocacy.

So how do you go about setting and maintaining boundaries in a way that feels authentic and empowering? Let's explore some practical strategies.

Solution #1: Understand Your Boundaries

The first step in setting effective boundaries is getting clear on what your boundaries actually are. This may seem obvious, but many of us have never taken the time to really think about what we need and want in our relationships and interactions.

One way to start identifying your boundaries is to pay attention to your gut reactions. Notice when you feel resentful, anxious, or overwhelmed in response to someone else's words or actions. These uncomfortable emotions are often a sign that a boundary has been crossed or needs to be set.

For example, let's say you have a coworker who consistently interrupts you during meetings or takes credit for your ideas. You may feel irritated, disrespected, or even angry in these moments. That's a clue that you need to set a boundary around communication and collaboration.

Or perhaps you have a friend who frequently cancels plans at the last minute or shows up late without apology. You may feel hurt, disappointed, or taken for granted. That's a sign that you need to set a boundary around reliability and respect for your time.

Another way to identify your boundaries is to reflect on your values and priorities. What's most important to you in your relationships and interactions? What do you need to feel safe, respected, and valued? What are your non-negotiables?

For instance, honesty and transparency may be top values for you. That means you need relationships where there's open communication and no hidden agendas. Or perhaps work–life balance is a key priority. That means you need to set boundaries around your availability outside of work hours and protect your personal time.

Some other common boundaries include:

- Physical boundaries: your personal space, privacy, and physical touch
- Emotional boundaries: your feelings, thoughts, and ability to separate your emotions from others'

- Time boundaries: how you spend your time, how much time you give to others, and how much alone time you need
- Material boundaries: your money, possessions, and resources
- Intellectual boundaries: your ideas, creativity, and credit for your work
- Sexual boundaries: your comfort level with sexual touch, activity, and communication

Everyone's boundaries will be different based on their unique needs, values, and experiences. What's important is that you take the time to reflect on what matters most to you and what you need to feel safe and supported.

Once you have a sense of your key boundaries, it can be helpful to write them down and refer back to them often. You might make a list of your "non-negotiables" or create a personal bill of rights. The more clarity and conviction you have around your boundaries, the easier it will be to communicate and uphold them.

Solution #2: Setting Boundaries

Once you know what your boundaries are, the next step is actually setting them. This means communicating your limits and needs clearly and directly to others.

Setting boundaries can feel scary at first, especially if you're not used to standing up for yourself. You may worry about coming across as rude or aggressive, or fear that others will reject or abandon you if you say no.

But remember, setting boundaries is not about controlling others or making them change. It's about taking responsibility for your own well-being and communicating what you need to thrive. When you set boundaries from a place of clarity and compassion, others are more likely to respond positively and respectfully.

Here are some tips for setting effective boundaries:

- **Be direct and specific.** Avoid hinting, hedging, or apologizing for your needs. Use clear, concise language to state your boundary firmly and kindly. For example, instead of saying, "I'm sorry, I'm just so busy lately," try, "I appreciate the invitation, but I'm not available to take on any new commitments right now."
- **Use "I" statements.** Focus on expressing your own needs and feelings rather than blaming or attacking others. For instance, instead of saying, "You always take advantage of me," try, "I feel overwhelmed when I'm asked to take on last-minute requests. I need more advance notice to plan my time effectively."
- **Be consistent.** Boundaries only work if you enforce them consistently. If you set a boundary and then let it slide, others will learn that your limits are negotiable. It's important to follow through and hold firm, even if it feels uncomfortable at first.
- **Start small.** If you're new to setting boundaries, it's okay to start with small, low-stakes requests and work your way up. For example, you might practice saying no to a minor request from a coworker before tackling a more challenging conversation with a family member.
- **Expect some pushback.** Not everyone will be thrilled about your new boundaries, and that's okay. Some people may try to guilt trip you, argue with you, or ignore your requests altogether. Remember, their reaction is not your

responsibility. Stay focused on what you need and trust that the right people will respect your limits.

- **Seek support.** Setting and maintaining boundaries can be tough, especially if you have a history of people-pleasing or codependency. Don't be afraid to seek support from a therapist, coach, or trusted friend as you navigate this new terrain. Having a cheerleader in your corner can make all the difference.

It's also important to remember that boundaries are not a one-time conversation. They require ongoing communication and reinforcement. As your needs and circumstances change, your boundaries may need to evolve as well. Be willing to reassess and adjust as needed, and keep the lines of communication open with the people in your life.

Solution #3: (Re)enforcing Boundaries

Even with the best of intentions and the clearest of communication, there will be times when others cross your boundaries. Maybe a friend keeps showing up unannounced, or a coworker continues to send you non-urgent emails on the weekends. When this happens, it's important to have strategies in place for reinforcing your limits and protecting your well-being.

The first step is to recognize when a boundary has been violated. Pay attention to your emotions and physical sensations. Do you feel resentful, anxious, or drained? Is your jaw clenched or your stomach in knots? These are all signs that someone may have overstepped your limits.

Once you've identified that a boundary has been crossed, it's important to address it as soon as possible. The longer you wait, the harder it will be to speak up and the more likely you are to harbor resentment or let the behavior continue unchecked.

When communicating about a boundary violation, use the same clear, direct language you used when setting the boundary in the first place. Avoid blaming or attacking, and focus on expressing your own needs and expectations.

For example, let's say your partner has a habit of interrupting you when you're trying to focus on work. You've set a boundary around your need for uninterrupted work time, but they keep barging in with questions or comments. Here's how you might address it:

"I know you don't mean to disrupt me, but when you come into my office while I'm working, it breaks my concentration and makes it harder for me to focus. I need you to respect my work time and wait until I'm available to talk unless it's an emergency. Can we agree on a signal that I'm not to be disturbed, like closing my office door?"

Notice how this response is firm but kind. It acknowledges the other person's intentions while clearly restating the boundary and requesting a specific change in behavior.

Of course, not everyone will respond positively to boundary enforcement. Some people may get defensive, dismiss your concerns, or even lash out in anger. In these cases, it's important to stay grounded in your own truth and not take their reaction personally.

Remember, you are not responsible for other people's emotions or behavior. You are only responsible for communicating your needs clearly and consistently. If someone repeatedly disrespects your boundaries despite your best efforts, it may be time to reevaluate the relationship and consider whether it's serving your highest good.

In some cases, boundary violations may be more serious and require a stronger response. If someone is engaging in abusive, threatening, or illegal behavior, it's important to seek help and support from a trusted friend, therapist, or even law enforcement. Your safety and well-being should always be the top priority.

Ultimately, reinforcing boundaries is a practice of self-love and self-respect. It's about honoring your own needs and trusting that you are worthy of being treated with dignity and care. The more you practice upholding your limits, the easier and more natural it will become.

Wrapping Up...

Setting and maintaining boundaries is a crucial skill for cultivating mental toughness and resilience. When you know your limits and communicate them clearly, you create a sense of safety and security that allows you to thrive in all areas of life.

Remember, boundaries are not about being selfish or uncaring. They're about taking responsibility for your own well-being and creating the conditions for healthy, mutually fulfilling relationships. By honoring your own needs and desires, you model self-respect and self-advocacy for others.

To recap, the three keys to effective boundary setting are:

- Understanding your boundaries: taking the time to reflect on your values, needs, and limits
- Setting your boundaries: communicating your limits clearly, directly, and consistently

- Reinforcing your boundaries: addressing violations promptly and firmly and seeking support when needed

With practice and patience, setting and maintaining boundaries will become second nature. You'll find yourself feeling more grounded, empowered, and resilient in the face of life's challenges.

But boundaries are just one piece of the mental toughness puzzle. In the next chapter, we'll explore another crucial component: cultivating a positive, optimistic mindset. Get ready to harness the power of your thoughts and beliefs to create the life you truly desire.

Case Study: Emily

Emily was a kind-hearted and hardworking nurse who always went above and beyond for her patients and colleagues. She regularly stayed late to cover shifts, took on extra tasks without complaint, and was the go-to person for emotional support in her unit. While her dedication was admirable, it was also taking a serious toll on her well-being.

Emily was constantly exhausted, both physically and emotionally. She had little time for her own self-care practices or hobbies, and her relationships outside of work were suffering. She frequently felt resentful and unappreciated, but she didn't know how to say no or advocate for her own needs.

One day, after a particularly grueling shift, Emily broke down in tears in the break room. Her supervisor, who had noticed Emily's increasing stress levels, sat down with her and gently asked what was going on. Through sobs, Emily shared how overwhelmed and depleted she felt, as if she were pouring from an empty cup.

Emily's supervisor listened with compassion and then asked a powerful question: "What boundaries do you need to set to take better care of yourself?" This question stopped Emily in her tracks. She had never really thought about her own boundaries before, always putting others' needs before her own.

With her supervisor's encouragement, Emily started to reflect on what she needed to feel more balanced and resilient. She realized that she needed to limit her overtime hours, take regular breaks during her shifts, and be more selective about which extra tasks she took on. She also recognized that she needed to carve out more time for her personal life and self-care.

Armed with this new self-awareness, Emily began to communicate her boundaries more clearly and consistently. When a colleague asked her to cover an extra shift at the last minute, she kindly but firmly explained that she had already made plans for her day off and couldn't accommodate the request. When a patient's family member started to vent excessively about personal issues, Emily gently redirected the conversation and suggested some counseling resources.

At first, setting these boundaries felt awkward and uncomfortable for Emily. She worried that others would see her as selfish or uncaring. However, as she practiced expressing her limits with respect and compassion, she found that most people were understanding and supportive. In fact, many of her colleagues expressed admiration for her self-advocacy and started to follow her lead in setting their own boundaries.

Over time, Emily began to notice significant improvements in her well-being and resilience. With more time for rest, self-care, and personal pursuits, she had more energy and focus at work. She was able to be more fully present with her patients and colleagues without the underlying resentment or depletion she had previously felt.

Emily's boundaries also had a positive ripple effect on her relationships outside of work. She was able to be a more attentive and supportive partner, friend, and family member because she wasn't constantly drained by overextending herself. She even inspired some of her loved ones to examine and communicate their own boundaries more effectively.

Of course, setting and maintaining boundaries wasn't always easy for Emily. There were times when people pushed back against her limits or tried to make her feel guilty for prioritizing her own needs. In these moments, Emily had to dig deep and remind herself that her boundaries were not only valid but necessary for her long-term health and happiness.

Through her journey, Emily learned that boundaries are not about building walls or shutting others out. They're about creating the conditions for more authentic, sustainable, and mutually nourishing relationships. By honoring her own limits and needs, she was able to show up more fully and compassionately for the people and causes she cared about most.

Emily's story is a powerful reminder that setting boundaries is not selfish but an act of self-love and respect. When we have the courage to communicate our needs and limits clearly, we create space for greater joy, connection, and resilience in all areas of our lives. With practice and patience, we can all learn to set and maintain the boundaries we need to thrive.

EIGHT

Step #7: Positivity Powers— Cultivating Optimism

 It is not the mountain we conquer but ourselves.

Edmund Hillary

In this final step of our 7-step journey to mental toughness, we turn to one of the most powerful tools in your arsenal: optimism. Optimism isn't just about putting on a happy face —it's a fundamental way of perceiving and interacting with the world that has profound effects on your mental strength and well-being. In this chapter, you'll learn what it really means to be optimistic, the incredible benefits it bestows, and concrete strategies to cultivate an optimistic outlook, even in the face of adversity. By the end, you'll feel empowered to harness the power of positivity to enhance your mental toughness like never before.

The Power of Optimism

What exactly is optimism? At its core, optimism is the belief that things will generally work out for the best. It's a positive mindset that interprets experiences, events, and the future in a hopeful, confident light. Optimists tend to view challenges as temporary setbacks rather than permanent disasters. They believe in their ability to overcome obstacles and expect good things to happen.

This positive outlook isn't just feel-good fluff—optimism has measurable benefits for both mental and physical health. Research (Conversano et al., 2010) has linked optimism to

- lower rates of depression and anxiety
- better coping skills during hardships and times of stress
- improved cardiovascular health and immune function
- longer life span and greater overall well-being

Optimism acts as a buffer against life's inevitable difficulties. When you expect positive outcomes, you're more likely to take productive actions and persist in the face of challenges. In contrast, pessimists tend to give up more easily and slip into passivity or despair.

In terms of mental toughness specifically, optimism is like rocket fuel. It enables you to

- persevere through setbacks, disappointments, and failures
- bounce back from adversity with renewed determination
- maintain confidence and motivation when the going gets tough
- find creative solutions and opportunities amid obstacles

With an optimistic mindset, you stay focused on possibilities rather than dwelling on problems. You view hardships as temporary and specific rather than permanent and pervasive. This allows you to maintain perspective and keep moving forward even when things are difficult.

Furthermore, optimism improves your life across the board. Research shows that compared to pessimists, optimists tend to

- earn higher incomes and experience greater career success
- have more satisfying, trusting, and long-lasting relationships
- be viewed as more likable, charismatic, and influential by others
- enjoy better physical health and recover faster from illness/injury
- experience greater happiness, well-being, and overall life satisfaction

Because optimists expect positive outcomes, they're more likely to take calculated risks and keep striving toward their goals rather than giving up prematurely. They also tend to invest in their relationships, take care of their health, and make choices that create self-fulfilling prophecies of success and well-being.

Overall, tapping into the power of optimism is one of the most effective ways to upgrade your mental strength and quality of life. Optimism creates an upward spiral of positive thoughts, feelings, behaviors, and outcomes. It's not about ignoring reality or denying negative aspects of a situation. Rather, it's about intentionally shifting your focus toward what is good, what is possible, and what you can control. Here's how to cultivate this transformative mindset:

Solution #1: Honing a Positive Mindset

If you tend to be more of a "glass half empty" kind of thinker, don't despair—you absolutely can train your brain to be more positive.

It just takes consistent effort and practice to overcome entrenched negative thinking patterns.

The first step is to become aware of your explanatory style—the habitual ways in which you interpret and make sense of events. Pessimists have a negative explanatory style, characterized by the 3 P's:

- **Permanence:** Viewing negative situations as permanent and unchangeable. E.g., "I'll never find love because I'm unlovable."
- **Pervasiveness:** Globalizing negative events and allowing them to pervade all areas of life. E.g., "I failed that test, which means I'm a failure in general."
- **Personalization:** Blaming oneself and taking things personally. E.g., "It's all my fault that the project failed."

To shift toward a more positive mindset, practice catching and reframing these types of thoughts:

- Challenge permanence by reminding yourself that most situations are temporary. Look for examples of how you've overcome similar challenges before or how others have navigated this type of situation successfully. Ask yourself, "How might this change or resolve over time?"
- Combat pervasiveness by keeping things in perspective. Recognize that one negative event doesn't have to dictate your entire life experience. Compartmentalize by identifying areas of your life that are going well despite this adversity. Ask yourself, "What parts of my life are still good right now?"
- Reduce personalization by considering external factors and cutting yourself some slack. Acknowledge your role in

the situation without engaging in self-blame. Practice self-compassion and talk to yourself like a good friend would. Ask yourself, "How did others or circumstances contribute to this situation?"

Another effective way to cultivate a positive mindset is to intentionally focus on the good. The human brain is wired to pay more attention to negative stimuli (it's an evolutionary survival mechanism), but you can consciously override this tendency by

- regularly expressing gratitude, either privately or to others. Make a habit of noticing and appreciating the small joys, comforts, and privileges in your daily life.
- celebrating your own and others' successes, milestones, and efforts. Take time to acknowledge progress and give yourself credit for showing up.
- looking for the humor, beauty, inspiration, and humanity around you. Be on the lookout for small moments of delight throughout your day.
- surrounding yourself with positive people, messaging, and environments as much as possible. Curate your social media feed, reading material, and friend circles to be more uplifting than draining.

With repetition, you can shift your default thought patterns from negative to positive. It's like building a muscle—the more you practice optimistic thinking, the stronger and more automatic it becomes. Over time, your mind will start to scan for and expect the good, creating a self-reinforcing cycle of positivity.

Solution #2: Developing Optimism

In addition to generally honing a more positive mindset, you can proactively develop your optimism skills. The key lies in how you explain events to yourself and others.

Optimists view negative events as temporary, limited in scope, and influenced by external factors rather than solely caused by personal failings. You can develop a more optimistic mindset by challenging pessimistic thoughts, considering multiple contributing factors, and recognizing the impermanence of most situations.

Now, let's shift our focus to actionable techniques for cultivating optimism and seeing the bright side in the rest of this solution section.

With practice, your explanatory style will shift, and your capacity for optimism will grow. You'll be able to metabolize adversity more quickly and reframe challenges in a more hopeful, empowering light.

Another key optimism skill is finding the bright side or silver lining in difficult situations. Even in truly tragic circumstances, optimists look for

- glimmers of goodness, beauty, or meaning
- opportunities for growth, learning, or positive change
- things to be grateful for amid the pain and difficulty

This isn't about minimizing or denying the negative—it's about maintaining a balanced perspective. It's about recognizing that even in the darkest of times, there are still sources of light and reasons for hope.

Regularly ask yourself questions like:

- "What valuable lessons or insights might I gain from this experience?"
- "How might I use this situation as an opportunity to build a new skill or manifest a positive change?"
- "What am I discovering about my own strength, resilience, and capabilities?"
- "What am I grateful for, even in the midst of this challenge?"

Make a habit of noticing and naming the positive aspects of tough situations, no matter how small. The more you flex this optimism muscle, the more easily your mind will find the good—even on the darkest of days.

Solution #3: Optimism vs. Toxic Positivity

As you cultivate an optimistic mindset, it's important to avoid veering into the territory of toxic positivity. Genuine optimism means maintaining a realistically positive outlook while still acknowledging the full spectrum of human emotions and experiences. Toxic positivity, in contrast, is an overly simplified, one-dimensional approach that denies, minimizes, or invalidates anything perceived as negative.

Toxic positivity shows up as

- feeling guilty or ashamed for experiencing painful emotions
- suppressing or denying anger, sadness, grief, fear, etc.
- insisting on being happy and upbeat all the time
- shaming others for expressing negativity or vulnerability

- offering unhelpful platitudes like "Just stay positive!"
- avoiding difficult conversations or situations

While well-intentioned, toxic positivity can do more harm than good. It stigmatizes normal, healthy human emotions and pressures people to be inauthentic. It also prevents genuine processing of challenging experiences, which is essential for healing and growth.

Genuine optimism, on the other hand

- makes room for the full range of human emotions
- validates that it's normal and okay to feel pain/negativity sometimes
- encourages processing challenging feelings with self-compassion
- offers hope and encouragement without denying current realities
- remains forward-looking while still acknowledging the present
- focuses on what's within your control and influence

To cultivate authentic optimism without sliding into toxic positivity:

- Acknowledge the reality of your current situation and how you feel about it. Resist the urge to sugar-coat or gloss over real challenges.
- Validate your own and others' difficult emotions with understanding and compassion. Let yourself feel your feelings without judgment.

- Express challenging emotions in healthy ways, like journaling, having honest conversations with trusted confidantes, creating art or music, etc.
- Gently redirect your mind toward positive possibilities and solutions once you've processed the initial wave of emotion. Ask yourself what beneficial actions you can take or changes you can make.
- Offer realistic hope and encouragement to yourself and others. Share messages that are empowering without being dismissive or overly simplistic.

It's a delicate dance, but with practice, you can master the balance of acknowledging difficulty while maintaining an optimistic outlook. You'll learn how to metabolize adversity with self-compassion and grace, using challenges as fuel for growth and transformation.

Optimism In Action

The inspiring story of POW Admiral James Stockdale perfectly illustrates the power of realistic optimism. Admiral Stockdale was held captive and tortured for eight years during the Vietnam War. Despite unimaginable suffering, he managed to survive the ordeal with his spirit intact and even thrive in the later years of his life.

When asked about his coping strategy in prison, Stockdale explained that he balanced realism with hope. He said "I never lost faith in the end of the story. I never doubted not only that I would get out but also that I would prevail in the end and turn the experience into the defining event of my life, which, in retrospect, I would not trade."

At the same time, Stockdale didn't indulge in blind optimism or wishful thinking. When asked, "Who didn't make it out?" he replied, "Oh, that's easy. The optimists. They were the ones who said, 'We're going to be out by Christmas.' And Christmas would come, and Christmas would go. Then they'd say, 'We're going to be out by Easter.' And Easter would come, and Easter would go. And then Thanksgiving, and then it would be Christmas again. And they died of a broken heart."

Stockdale's experience highlights the sweet spot of genuine optimism—having faith in the end of the story while also confronting current realities. It's about holding the tension between accepting what is and expecting the best moving forward. It's remaining realistically hopeful while taking full responsibility for your circumstances.

So, how can we apply the "Stockdale Paradox" in our own lives? Here are some key lessons:

- **Acknowledge the brutal facts of your current reality.** Don't deny or minimize challenges, setbacks, or painful emotions. Confront the truth head-on.
- **At the same time, maintain unwavering faith that you will ultimately prevail.** Hold onto hope and optimism even in the darkest times. Visualize the end of your story.
- **Focus on what's within your control.** Accept what you can't change and take responsibility for what you can influence. Channel your energy into positive action.
- **Find meaning and purpose in adversity.** Look for ways to learn, grow, and become a better version of yourself. Use challenges as opportunities for transformation.
- **Stay connected to your reasons for hope.** Regularly remind yourself of your strengths, values, and long-term vision. Surround yourself with relationships and resources that fuel your optimism.

By holding both realism and optimism simultaneously, you'll build authentic mental toughness—the ability to acknowledge difficulties while maintaining an empowered, proactive mindset. You'll learn to metabolize adversity into fuel for your growth and ultimate success.

Wrapping Up...

In this chapter, we explored the transformative power of optimism in cultivating unshakable mental strength and resilience. By understanding the true nature of optimism, its incredible benefits, and practical strategies for honing a positive mindset, you've gained a powerful tool to navigate life's challenges with grace and determination.

Throughout this chapter, we've covered a wealth of tools and techniques to increase your optimism, including:

- Understanding the true nature of optimism, its incredible benefits, and practical strategies for honing a positive mindset to cultivate a realistic yet hopeful outlook.
- Intentionally shifting your focus toward what is good, possible, and controllable while approaching challenges as opportunities for learning, transformation, and staying connected to your deepest values and purpose.
- Celebrating progress, radiating positivity and resilience, and inspiring others to create a ripple effect of positive change and empowerment.

Optimism is the cornerstone that ties all these skills together. By maintaining a realistic yet hopeful outlook, you'll be able to leverage your full mental and emotional capacity to overcome obstacles, learn from setbacks, and keep moving forward with unwavering determination.

As you integrate the practices and mindset shifts covered in this chapter, remember that optimism is not about denying reality or suppressing difficult emotions. Rather, it's about intentionally shifting your focus toward what is good, what is possible, and what you can control. It's about having faith in your ability to handle whatever comes your way and trusting in your capacity for growth and resilience.

Cultivating authentic optimism is a lifelong journey of choosing thoughts, beliefs, and actions that empower you to be your best self. It's about approaching challenges as opportunities for learning and transformation, staying connected to your deepest values and purpose, and inspiring others with your hopefulness and tenacity.

As you continue to flex your optimism muscle and build mental toughness, celebrate each milestone and moment of progress along the way. Remember that you already have everything you need to create a life of authentic joy, meaning, and fulfillment. Keep expecting the best while taking full responsibility for your circumstances. Stay realistically hopeful and fiercely committed to your personal growth and success.

Your optimism is a gift to yourself and to the world around you. As you radiate positivity and resilience in the face of life's challenges, you'll inspire others to rise to their highest potential as well.

The journey of mental toughness is one of continual evolution and expansion. With each challenge you overcome, each setback you learn from, and each victory you celebrate, you'll discover new depths of strength, wisdom, and resilience within yourself.

Case Study: Jasmine

Jasmine had always been a worrywart, even as a child. She constantly fretted about worst-case scenarios, from natural disasters to failing grades to social rejection. As an adult, her pessimism had become a self-fulfilling prophecy. She'd been passed over for promotions at work, had a string of unfulfilling relationships, and generally felt like she was just scraping by in life.

Jasmine's pessimism was a major factor in her struggles. She tended to blow small setbacks way out of proportion, turning minor annoyances into catastrophes in her mind. She obsessed over what was going wrong while ignoring her strengths and accomplishments. Over time, she'd developed a deep-seated belief that good things just didn't happen for her. Her motivation and confidence were at an all-time low.

One day, after yet another disappointment, Jasmine stumbled across a book on mental toughness. The chapter on optimism struck a chord. She recognized herself in the descriptions of pessimistic thinking and realized how much her negative outlook had been holding her back. She resolved to start training her brain for positivity.

At first, it felt forced and phony to look for the bright side. Jasmine's mind was so used to going down disastrous rabbit holes. But she was determined to rewire her thinking. She started a daily gratitude journal, listing at least three good things about each day, no matter how small. She caught herself catastrophizing and consciously replaced those thoughts with more realistic ones. For example, instead of "I'm going to bomb this presentation and get fired," she'd think, "I've prepared thoroughly, and even if it doesn't go perfectly, I'll survive and learn from it."

Jasmine also practiced reframing challenges as opportunities. When she was passed up for a promotion, instead of spiraling into despair, she thought, "This is a chance to get feedback on where I can improve so I'm in an even stronger position next time." When her car broke down, she told herself, "I can handle this. It's a hassle, but I'll figure it out, and maybe I'll discover a great new mechanic in the process."

Slowly but surely, Jasmine's default way of viewing the world started to shift. It became more natural to find the silver linings and expect positive outcomes. She felt lighter, more hopeful, and energetic. Her newfound optimism gave her the courage to take on challenges she would have shied away from before. She applied for a stretch role at work and got it. She said yes to new social opportunities and expanded her circle of friends.

As Jasmine's life started to transform for the better, she realized how much her past pessimism had been clouding her perceptions. Had the world changed? Or had her view of it changed? Sure, bad things still happen sometimes, but she no longer let them define her. She could acknowledge negativity without getting lost in it. Her newfound optimism was like a buoy, allowing her to ride the waves of life's ups and downs with so much more ease and confidence.

There were moments when Jasmine caught herself sliding back into old negative thought patterns. When this happened, she knew she had to be deliberate about shifting her mindset. She'd take some deep breaths, recall her gratitude list, and gently steer her thoughts in a more optimistic direction. Sometimes, she'd reach out to an encouraging friend or do something kind for someone else, both guaranteed mood boosters.

Over time, Jasmine realized that optimism wasn't about denying life's difficulties; it was about choosing a life-giving perspective in the midst of them. Her positive outlook became a source of incredible resilience, allowing her to rebound from setbacks and keep striving toward her goals with confidence and hope.

No, her life wasn't perfect. Yes, she still felt pessimistic sometimes. But Jasmine had learned how to catch and reframe those thoughts before they could spiral out of control. She'd discovered that her mindset was a powerful tool she could use to shape her experience of the world. And as she focused more and more on the good, the good just kept growing.

NINE

Bonus Chapter—Assertiveness Training 101

 Out of difficulties grow miracles.

Jean de la Bruyere

Throughout our journey of mastering mental toughness, we've explored a wide array of strategies and techniques to help you cultivate unshakable resilience and inner strength. From overcoming overthinking to honing emotional agility to practicing optimism, you now have a robust toolkit to navigate life's challenges with grace and determination.

In this bonus chapter, we'll dive into one final skill that can take your mental toughness to the next level: assertiveness. Assertiveness is the ability to express your thoughts, feelings, and needs in a clear, direct, and respectful manner. It's about standing up for yourself, setting healthy boundaries, and communicating with confidence and integrity.

When you're assertive, you're able to advocate for your wants and needs without resorting to aggression or passivity. You can handle difficult conversations and conflicts with poise and effectiveness, staying true to yourself while also respecting others. Assertiveness is a key component of mental toughness because it allows you to navigate interpersonal challenges with courage, resilience, and self-assuredness.

In this chapter, you'll learn the core principles and techniques of assertiveness training, a powerful approach to building assertiveness skills. We'll explore the benefits of being assertive, common barriers to assertiveness, and practical strategies you can start using today to communicate with greater clarity, confidence, and impact. By the end of this chapter, you'll have everything you need to assert yourself effectively in any situation, from the boardroom to the living room.

What Is Assertiveness Training?

At its core, assertiveness training is a type of behavior therapy designed to help individuals develop the skills to express their thoughts, feelings, and needs in a direct, honest, and appropriate way. It's about learning to communicate with confidence and respect, setting healthy boundaries, and standing up for oneself without resorting to aggression, manipulation, or passivity.

Assertiveness training typically involves a combination of cognitive, emotional, and behavioral techniques, such as:

- identifying and challenging limiting beliefs and assumptions
- practicing self-awareness and emotional regulation
- developing effective communication skills, both verbal and nonverbal
- roleplaying difficult conversations and scenarios
- setting and maintaining healthy boundaries

- cultivating a growth mindset and self-acceptance

Through assertiveness training, individuals learn to replace passive, aggressive, or passive-aggressive communication styles with assertive ones. They develop the confidence to express themselves authentically and the resilience to handle conflicts and negotiations with grace and effectiveness.

Benefits of Assertiveness Training

Developing assertiveness skills through training can have a profound impact on various aspects of life. Some of the key benefits include:

- **Improved communication and relationships:** Assertiveness enables you to express your needs and boundaries clearly, reducing misunderstandings and conflicts in personal and professional relationships.
- **Greater self-confidence and self-esteem:** By learning to stand up for yourself and communicate your worth, you develop a stronger sense of self-assurance and self-respect.
- **Enhanced decision-making and problem-solving abilities:** Assertiveness training teaches you to think critically, express your opinions confidently, and find win-win solutions in challenging situations.
- **Reduced stress and anxiety:** When you're able to advocate for your needs and manage conflicts effectively, you experience less stress and worry in interpersonal interactions.
- **Increased resilience and adaptability:** Assertiveness skills enable you to handle difficult people and situations with greater ease, bounce back from setbacks, and adapt to change more effectively.

- **Greater authenticity and integrity:** By communicating honestly and directly, you stay true to your values and build trust and respect with others.
- **Enhanced leadership and influence:** Assertive individuals are seen as more credible, charismatic, and persuasive, making them more effective leaders and change agents.

Overall, assertiveness training can help you communicate with greater clarity, confidence, and impact, improving your relationships, well-being, and success in all areas of life.

How Assertiveness Training Improves Mental Toughness

In addition to its many personal and interpersonal benefits, assertiveness training is also a powerful tool for building mental toughness. When you're assertive, you're better able to do the following:

- **Handle difficult conversations and conflicts:** With assertiveness skills, you can navigate tense interactions with composure, staying focused on solutions rather than getting derailed by emotions.
- **Advocate for yourself and your ideas:** Assertiveness empowers you to speak up for what you believe in, even in the face of opposition or skepticism, fostering greater resilience and persistence.
- **Manage stress and adversity effectively:** By communicating your needs and managing conflicts proactively, you're better equipped to handle life's challenges and bounce back from setbacks.
- **Develop greater self-awareness and emotional intelligence:** Assertiveness training requires you to tune

into your own thoughts, feelings, and values, as well as those of others, fostering greater empathy and adaptability.

- **Cultivate a growth mindset and self-acceptance:** Through assertiveness training, you learn to embrace your strengths and weaknesses, take risks, learn from failures, and communicate with authenticity and self-compassion.

In essence, assertiveness is a key pillar of mental toughness because it allows you to navigate interpersonal challenges with courage, resilience, and grace. By learning to express yourself clearly, set healthy boundaries, and advocate for your needs, you develop the inner strength and flexibility to thrive in the face of any obstacle.

Solution #1: Communication

At the heart of assertiveness training is effective communication. To express yourself assertively, you need to be able to articulate your thoughts, feelings, and needs in a clear, direct, and respectful manner. This requires a combination of self-awareness, emotional intelligence, and practical communication skills.

Assessing Your Style

The first step in improving your assertiveness is to assess your current communication style. Are you more passive, aggressive, passive-aggressive, or assertive? Consider how you typically express yourself in different situations, such as:

- giving and receiving feedback
- expressing disagreement or dissatisfaction
- making requests or saying no

288 • AMBER PRESTON

- negotiating or resolving conflicts
- standing up for your ideas or beliefs

You can take self-assessments or ask for feedback from trusted friends or colleagues to get a better sense of your communication strengths and areas for improvement. Some common communication styles include:

- **Passive:** avoids expressing thoughts and feelings; goes along with others' demands; fears conflict and rejection
- **Aggressive:** expresses thoughts and feelings in a hostile, threatening way; disregards others' needs and rights
- **Passive-aggressive:** expresses thoughts and feelings indirectly through sarcasm, sabotage, or non-compliance; fears direct confrontation
- **Assertive:** expresses thoughts and feelings in an honest, direct, and respectful way; considers own and others' needs; communicates with confidence and clarity

By understanding your default communication style, you can start to identify patterns and triggers that may be holding you back from being more assertive.

Communicating Assertively

To communicate assertively, practice expressing yourself in an honest, direct, and respectful manner. Use "I" statements to take ownership of your thoughts and feelings rather than blaming or accusing others. For example:

- Instead of "You always interrupt me and don't let me finish," say, "I feel disrespected when I'm interrupted. I need to be able to express my thoughts fully."

- Instead of "Your idea won't work," say, "I have concerns about the feasibility of that approach. Can we explore some alternative solutions?"
- Focus on being specific, objective, and solution-oriented in your communication. Avoid generalizations, exaggerations, or personal attacks. Use a calm, confident tone of voice and maintain open, engaged body language.

When communicating assertively, it's also important to listen actively and empathetically to others. Show that you hear and understand their perspective, even if you disagree. Look for win-win solutions that consider everyone's needs and concerns.

Some key phrases for assertive communication include:

- "I think/feel/need..."
- "What are your thoughts on..."
- "My understanding is... Is that accurate?"
- "How can we resolve this in a way that works for both of us?"
- "I appreciate your perspective. Here's another way of looking at it..."
- Saying "No"

One of the most important assertiveness skills is the ability to say no respectfully. As we talked about back in Chapter 7, setting and maintaining healthy boundaries is essential for protecting your time, energy, and well-being. When someone makes a request or demand that doesn't align with your needs or values, practice expressing your limits clearly and firmly.

For example:

- "I appreciate you thinking of me for this project, but I don't have the bandwidth to take on any extra commitments right now."
- "I understand you're in a tight spot, but I'm not comfortable lending money. Let's brainstorm some other resources that could help."
- "I know you're eager to spend more time together, but I need some alone time this weekend to recharge. How about we plan something for next week?"

Remember that saying no doesn't make you selfish or uncaring. It's a sign of self-respect and personal integrity. By setting boundaries assertively, you create the space to focus on what truly matters to you and show up as your best self in your relationships and responsibilities.

Solution #2: Body Language

In addition to verbal communication, nonverbal cues also play a significant role in assertiveness. Your body language, facial expressions, and tone of voice can reinforce or undermine your message, affecting how others perceive and respond to you. By aligning your nonverbal communication with your assertive intentions, you can convey confidence, credibility, and respect in any interaction.

How Body Language Improves Communication

Research shows that nonverbal cues account for a significant portion of our communication impact. Some studies suggest that body language and tone of voice convey over 90% of our message, while the actual words account for less than 10% (Park & Park, 2018).

When your nonverbal communication aligns with your verbal message, it enhances your overall effectiveness and persuasiveness. Confident, open body language signals that you believe in what you're saying and can be trusted. On the other hand, closed or submissive body language can undermine your credibility and authority, even if your words are assertive.

Some key body language cues that can improve your assertive communication include:

- maintaining good eye contact (without staring or glaring)
- standing or sitting up straight with your shoulders back
- keeping your arms uncrossed and your hands visible
- using open, expansive gestures to emphasize key points
- smiling genuinely to convey warmth and friendliness
- nodding to show understanding and engagement
- mirroring the other person's body language to build rapport

Open vs. Closed Body Language

In assertiveness training, it's important to understand the difference between open and closed body language. Open body language conveys confidence, receptivity, and engagement, while closed body language signals defensiveness, resistance, or disinterest.

Examples of open body language include:

- facing the person you're speaking with directly
- maintaining an open, upright posture

- keeping your arms and legs uncrossed
- making appropriate eye contact
- using fluid, expansive gestures

In contrast, closed body language may involve:

- crossing your arms or legs tightly
- hunching or slouching
- avoiding eye contact or looking down
- fidgeting or tapping nervously
- turning your body away from the other person

To communicate assertively, aim to adopt an open, engaged posture that signals your confidence and receptivity. Avoid defensive or submissive stances that may undermine your message.

Body Language for Assertiveness

In addition to general open and engaging body language, there are specific nonverbal cues that can enhance your assertiveness in communication:

- Stand or sit up straight, with your shoulders back and your head held high. This posture conveys confidence and self-assurance.
- Make direct eye contact, holding the other person's gaze for a few seconds at a time. This signals your engagement and sincerity.
- Use expansive, purposeful gestures to emphasize key points. For example, you might use your hands to indicate size or importance, or point to visual aids.

- Speak in a clear, steady voice, enunciating your words and varying your tone and inflection to add impact. Avoid mumbling, trailing off, or speaking too quickly.
- Maintain a neutral or pleasant facial expression, smiling warmly when appropriate. Avoid scowling, frowning, or rolling your eyes, which can come across as aggressive or dismissive.
- Take up space by standing or sitting with your feet shoulder-width apart and your arms relaxed at your sides. Avoid making yourself small or constricted.

Remember, the goal is to convey confidence, openness, and respect through your body language. By aligning your nonverbal cues with your assertive message, you reinforce your credibility and effectiveness in any interaction.

Solution #3: Emotional Management

Effective assertiveness requires not only clear communication and confident body language but also emotional intelligence and self-regulation. When you're able to manage your emotions effectively, you can stay grounded, focused, and respectful even in challenging or high-stakes situations. Emotional management is a key skill for assertiveness and overall mental toughness.

How Emotional Management Improves Assertiveness

Emotions play a powerful role in communication and relationships. When you're in touch with your own feelings and able to regulate them effectively, you're better able to

- express yourself clearly and authentically
- listen actively and empathetically to others

- stay calm and focused in the face of stress or conflict
- advocate for your needs and boundaries respectfully
- build and maintain trust and rapport with others

On the other hand, when emotions are running high and unchecked, they can derail even the most well-intentioned assertiveness efforts. Anger, fear, or defensiveness can lead to aggressive or passive-aggressive communication, while anxiety or self-doubt can result in passivity or avoidance.

By developing emotional intelligence and self-regulation skills, you can communicate assertively, even in emotionally charged situations. You're able to

- recognize and label your own emotions accurately
- understand the triggers and root causes of your feelings
- express your emotions in healthy, constructive ways
- manage stress and maintain composure under pressure
- empathize with and respond to others' emotions skillfully

Ultimately, emotional management allows you to approach challenging conversations and conflicts with greater clarity, confidence, and resilience. You're able to assert yourself effectively while also maintaining positive relationships and outcomes.

How to Regulate Emotions in Conversation

To communicate assertively in high-stakes or emotionally charged situations, try these strategies for regulating your emotions:

- **Take a pause and breathe deeply.** Before responding, take a few slow, deep breaths to calm your physiological arousal and clear your mind.

- **Label your emotions accurately.** Take a moment to identify what you're feeling without judgment. Naming your emotions helps to diffuse their intensity and gives you greater clarity and control.
- **Identify your triggers and hot buttons.** Notice what specific words, actions, or situations tend to provoke a strong emotional reaction in you. Anticipating these triggers can help you regulate your response more effectively.
- **Express your feelings constructively.** Use "I" statements to express your emotions in a clear, non-blaming way. For example, "I feel frustrated when..." or "I'm concerned about..."
- **Empathize with the other person's perspective.** Try to put yourself in the other person's shoes and understand their feelings and needs. Expressing empathy can help diffuse defensiveness and build rapport.
- **Focus on solutions and common ground.** Instead of getting stuck in emotional reactions, direct the conversation toward finding mutually beneficial solutions. Look for areas of agreement and shared goals.
- **Know when to take a break.** If emotions are running too high to have a productive conversation, suggest taking a break and returning to the discussion later. Use this time to process your feelings and regain your composure.

By practicing these emotional regulation strategies, you can assert yourself more effectively, even in challenging or contentious situations. You'll be able to express your needs and perspectives clearly while also maintaining your cool and building positive relationships.

Wrapping Up...

In this bonus chapter, we explored the power of assertiveness training for building mental toughness and resilience. By developing the skills to express yourself clearly, confidently, and respectfully, you can navigate any interpersonal challenge with greater ease and effectiveness.

We covered the key components of assertiveness training, including:

- assessing and improving your communication style
- practicing assertive verbal communication techniques
- aligning your body language with your assertive message
- managing your emotions effectively in high-stakes situations

Assertiveness is a crucial skill for mental toughness because it allows you to advocate for your needs, set healthy boundaries, and communicate with impact and integrity. When you're able to express yourself assertively, you build greater self-awareness, confidence, and resilience in all areas of life.

As we close out this comprehensive guide to mastering mental toughness, remember that building inner strength and resilience is an ongoing journey. Continue to practice and integrate the strategies and techniques covered in each chapter, from silencing your inner critic to cultivating optimism to communicating assertively. Stay committed to your personal growth and celebrate your progress along the way.

Conclusion

As we come to the end of our journey through the world of mental toughness, I hope you're feeling empowered, inspired, and equipped with the tools and strategies you need to build unshakable resilience and inner strength.

Throughout this book, we've explored the key components of mental toughness, from mastering your mindset to embracing challenges to communicating assertively. We've delved into the science behind peak performance and the psychology of resilience, and we've practiced proven techniques for overcoming adversity and achieving your goals.

You've learned how to silence your inner critic, cultivate optimism, and reframe setbacks as opportunities for growth. You've discovered the power of self-awareness, emotional agility, and healthy habits for managing stress and maintaining focus. Most importantly, you've gained the confidence and self-assurance to take bold action, speak your truth, and stay true to your values, no matter what obstacles come your way.

But remember, mastering mental toughness is not a one-time event but a lifelong journey of growth and self-discovery. It's about consistently choosing to show up as your best self, even in the face of fear, doubt, or adversity. It's about embracing the discomfort of change and the uncertainty of new challenges, knowing that this is where true strength and resilience are forged.

As you continue on your path to greater mental toughness, be patient and compassionate with yourself. Celebrate your progress, learn from your setbacks, and surround yourself with supportive people who inspire and challenge you to keep growing. Stay curious, stay committed, and stay true to your unique journey.

Remember, you are stronger than you know. You have the power to overcome any obstacle, achieve any goal, and create the life you desire. You have everything you need to thrive and succeed, not just in spite of challenges but because of them.

So keep honing your mental muscles, keep reaching for your highest potential, and keep shining your light in the world. Your mental toughness is not just a gift to yourself but to everyone around you, inspiring others with your courage, resilience, and unwavering spirit.

Thank you for joining me on this transformative journey of self-discovery and empowerment. It has been an honor to share these insights and strategies with you, and I hope they serve you well as you continue to master your mindset and unleash your inner strength.

Here's to your unbreakable mental toughness, your limitless potential, and your most fulfilling, purposeful life. Keep rising, keep shining, and keep embracing the power of your indomitable will. The world needs your unique brand of strength, resilience, and courage more than ever.

Share the Power of the 7-Step Transformation

As you turn the last pages of this book, I hope you are already feeling the powerful changes that arise when you take a proactive approach to your health and well-being. Habits take around 66 days to form, so make it a point to practice the strategies contained in this book until they form part of your daily life.

If this book has helped you feel more positive, set healthy boundaries, and prioritize your time, I hope you can share just one or two sentences about its impact on your life.

TAKE A MOMENT TO SHARE YOUR THOUGHTS!

Thanks once again. May you continue to feel empowered, inspired, and equipped to see every challenge as a vital opportunity for growth.

Scan the QR code to leave a review on Amazon!

References

Allende, I. (2024). *Isabel Allende quotes*. Southern Living. https://www.southernliving.com/culture/quotes-about-strength

Charney, D. S. (2003). The psychobiology of resilience and vulnerability to anxiety disorders: implications for prevention and treatment. *Dialogues in Clinical Neuroscience, 5*(3), 207–221. https://www.ncbi.nlm.nih.gov/pmc/articles/PMC3181630/

Conversano, C., Rotondo, A., Lensi, E., Della Vista, O., Arpone, F., & Reda, M. A. (2010). Optimism and its impact on mental and physical well-being. *Clinical Practice & Epidemiology in Mental Health, 6*(1), 25–29. https://doi.org/10.2174/1745017901006010025

Bruyere J. (2024). *Jean de la Bruyere quotes*. Southern Living. https://www.southernliving.com/culture/quotes-about-strength

Dweck, C. (2012). *Mindset: How you can fulfill your potential*. Robinson.

Gibran. K. (2024). *Khalil Gibran quotes*. Southern Living. https://www.southernliving.com/culture/quotes-about-strength

Hello Driven. *The 50 Best Resilience Quotes*. February 20, 2019. https://home.hellodriven.com/articles/the-50-best-resilience-quotes/

Hillary. E. (2024). *Edmund Hillary quotes*. Southern Living. https://www.southernliving.com/culture/quotes-about-strength

King, M.L. Jr. (2024). *Martin Luther King Jr. quotes*. Southern Living. https://www.southernliving.com/culture/quotes-about-strength

Lange, K. (2020, February 3). *Medal of honor Monday: Navy Vice Adm. James Stockdale*. U.S. Department of Defense. https://www.defense.gov/News/Feature-Stories/story/Article/2097870/medal-of-honor-monday-navy-vice-adm-james-stockdale/

Mandela, N. (2024). *Nelson Mandela quotes*. Southern Living. https://www.southernliving.com/culture/quotes-about-strength

Marley. B. (2024). *Bob Marley quotes*. Southern Living. https://www.southernliving.com/culture/quotes-about-strength

Park, S. G., & Park, K. H. (2018). Correlation between nonverbal communication and objective structured clinical examination score in medical students. *Korean Journal of Medical Education, 30*(3), 199–208. https://doi.org/10.3946/kjme.2018.94

Porter, C., Palmier-Claus, J., Branitsky, A., Mansell, W., Warwick, H., & Varese, F.

(2019). Childhood adversity and borderline personality disorder: a meta-analysis. *Acta Psychiatrica Scandinavica, 141*(1), 6–20. https://doi.org/10.1111/acps.13118

Uchtdorf, D. F. (2024). *Dieter F. Uchtdorf quotes*. Southern Living. https://www.southernliving.com/culture/quotes-about-strength

www.ingramcontent.com/pod-product-compliance
Lightning Source LLC
Chambersburg PA
CBHW030910120626
46554CB00001B/90